What entrepreneurs have to say...

Myth to Reality makes us understand that although we are successful according to industry standards, we have much more capacity to improve. Being the best requires the commitment and discipline explained in this book.
Gary Jackson, Pres. & CEO, Concord Companies, Inc., Mesa, AZ

Even from "Down Under" one can feel the touch in the heart, mind and soul of this uplifting, superb book. It deserves the highest recommendation to anyone who is contemplating, starting or running a new entrepreneurial business.
Peter R Kronborg, Co-Founder, Our People Plus, Melbourne, Australia

My business is becoming more & more a reflection of my life and how I've chosen to lead it.
Brian Fricke, Pres., Financial Management Concepts, Maitland, FL

Myth to Reality gives entrepreneurs the tools they need to take charge of their business and their life. Whether you've been in business for 20 years, 10 years, or are just starting out, this book will teach you how to work on your business, not in it.
Dom Vercamert, Pres., Strategic Financial Solutions, Charlotte, NC

Growing and running a successful business is an adventure — one that is driven by myth, spirit and vision. Myth to Reality offers four simple lessons that help understand the breadth and range of the entrepreneurial adventure.
Jerry Fulks, CEO, Fulks & Company, Seattle, WA

Myth to Reality challenges readers to find the passage of self-discovery that every successful entrepreneur must find.
Karen Conlon, President, California Assn. of Community Managers

How often have we heard of an entrepreneur starting out running a great business, only to end up with the business running him? McAlister and Burrows give their readers the insights and tools they need to make their business a reflection of their life and how they have chosen to lead it.
Dan Robertson, CEO, Robertson Industries, Phoenix, AZ

An exploration of business and individual growth. The book shows readers they are best able to transform their personal and professional passions and goals from myth into reality.
Mike Rubie, CEO, Mountain Supply Co., Missoula, MT

Myth to Reality

The Spirit of the Entrepreneurial Adventure

John McAlister & Jeff Burrows

Bridgewood Press
Phoenix, Arizona

Library of Congress Cataloging-in-Publication Data

McAlister, John, 1949-
   Myth to reality : the spirit of the entrepreneurial adventure /
by John McAlister & Jeff Burrows.
   p. cm.
Includes bibliographical references and index.
   ISBN 0-927015-30-7
1. New business enterprises. 2. Small business—Management.
3. Creative ability in business. 4. Entrepreneurship.
I. Burrows, Jeff, 1956- II. Title.

   HD62.5.M376 2003

   658.02′2—dc22

                              2003057881

Printed in the United States of America

Acknowledgements

In the family traditions I have been taught from childhood it is always good to give thanks and share appreciation with the people who have supported, encouraged, and tolerated my drive for excellence.

I especially want to thank my long time friend Elizabeth (Poppy) Potter who co-created with me the concepts of *Pathways, Passages, and Ceremonies.* Her dedication to the education and development of young people is tireless. She is a remarkable person.

Profound gratitude goes to my brother Doug McAlister for his support, ideas, and encouragement to complete this project. I hold him in the highest esteem. He is a brother of brothers and I will forever cherish our special relationship.

I am eternally grateful for my best of friends, Sandy Cohn. He is a tireless grammarian who slogged through our manuscript, ever vigilant and precisely critical. Jeannie Coates deserves honorable mention for her Herculean effort to do final edits with her sharp eyes and willingness to work in a short period of time.

Especially worthy of mention is Barbara Kerr, co-author of *Letters to the Medicine Man* and close friend. Her encouragement, coaching and support through countless drafts, cuts and edits, have been essential to the completion of a coherent book.

My brother Alan and his wife Janice, my sister Kate and her husband Michael Kupstas deserve special mention for their willingness to listen and help me put form to my ideas.

And I cannot forget my parents, C. R. and Mary Ann McAlister, who taught me their dedication to excellence. They bravely raised a creative and sometimes difficult child, dauntlessly teaching me to be the very best in all that I endeavor.

Michel Sarda of Bridgewood Press, publisher of wonderful books, believed in our effort to bridge spirit and business and brought our story into print. Both Jeff and I are especially thankful.

John McAlister

T
he person most directly responsible for this book becoming a reality is my wife Kim. Kim is my life partner and without her I would not have gone through the dramatic changes establishing healthy new boundaries in marriage, business, and my life. Trusting in relationship is an essential piece of our twenty-four year foundation together.

To my parents for always listening to my plans, loving me, telling me I had enormous potential, and celebrating when I reached new plateaus.

I thank John McAlister for listening to my story and agreeing to co-author this book.

The island of Maui and the sacred space Matt and Judy Montange shared with Kim and me during the last year of writing and editing.

Michael Gerber for his commitment to small business. Gratitude goes to all my original coaches: Stephen, Wendy, Janice, Shawn, and Shannon who taught me the strategy, the art, and the science of achieving my vision.

I have profound appreciation for all the members of Thunderlight Resources, past and present that teach me lessons about balanced leadership. I especially want to thank my long time friend Richard Olson for introducing me to the *E-Myth* process and my partner, Mick Heath. Without Mick I would not understand the laws of wealth and abundance nor have implemented them to serve my life and business.

To the business owners who dared to soar and change their life through our relationship I am grateful as a teacher, coach, guide, and most importantly, friend.

Jeff Burrows

*To all of you who have dared
to undertake the adventure, and to all of you
who will accept the challenge,
we dedicate this book.*

John McAlister and Jeff Burrows

Table of Contents

Introduction

Myth to Reality is written for business owners, CEOs, and senior executives who are actively pursuing the strategy, the art, and the science for achieving their personal vision in business and life. It is also of value for those who are at the threshold of starting a new business. It is for those people who have gathered their courage, moved out of the mainstream, and become business owners and senior managers. It is a practical guide with a singular purpose, which is to share knowledge distilled from many years of adventure and experience. This knowledge becomes explicit in four simple lessons of wisdom. Once understood and realized, these lessons form the context that can allow one to live to a full measure of his or her capacity, celebrate his or her achievements, and realize his or her dreams. The lessons deal succinctly with the issues of spirituality, myth, vision, and how they combine to influence in a positive way the reality of operating a business.

Our promise is to demonstrate to you how to eliminate obstacles, real and perceived, which are keeping you from reaching your full potential. It is a promise to share the principles for designing your business, so that it serves your life and the well being of the people who work with you. It is a promise to inspire you with stories and the successes of people who, with our coaching, have applied these principles.

Myth to Reality was born in early May of 2001, while we were sitting on Jeff's porch in sunny Arizona. We have been great friends for many years. Each of us in our own way managed to have success in business and to live life in the full richness of our families and our endeavors. Jeff began his career in financial planning and investment banking. Similarly, John started a career in the printing industry with Deluxe Corporation in the bank stationer business. Jeff left the brokerage, finance business, and founded Thunderlight Resources in 1993. In 2000, John ended a successful 30-year career and became a writer, a role that has taken him around the world as a lecturer on spirituality and business. As we looked into our futures, Jeff mentioned that he had always wanted to write a book about business and his life's journey. John followed by saying that he had had a similar desire. Thus, the idea for *Myth to Reality* was born. Jeff, rich with his years of experience coaching business owners, and John, with his corporate background in business development, product design, and management, launched the project. We committed ourselves to telling our stories, gleaned from our years of experience of making businesses successful. We insisted that our project produce an easy to read, understandable, and meaningful book that provides memorable ideas which inspire people to take action.

We want you to undertake this adventure with us. We call you to the adventure of your life. We will teach you how to occupy the space between your Spiritual Objective, your Mythic Story, and the Strategic Visions, which collectively drive the reality of doing your business.

Myth to Reality is about you and for you. It is for everyone who is responsible for creating and developing business, regardless of whether you own a business or work in the corporate world. It is a book that brings to light the necessary and vital principles of your spiritual significance and how they relate to orchestrating a business, so that you free yourself to accomplish all that you choose with excellence. The book will teach you to exercise proper attention, do strategic work, and learn what you need to know in order to create a balance of wealth, income, abundance, and freedom. It is a practical guide to understanding the breadth and range of the entrepreneurial adventure.

We know it works. *Myth to Reality* demonstrates how to focus on a new perspective toward becoming successful as an entrepreneur. Once the adventure is engaged, the pathway is clear, the passage of self-discovery begins. It is a passage that will dare the exploration and disclosure of a person's history in the search for purpose. The passage will reveal and clarify your vision of the future and how you want your business to serve your life and others. Business owners who have implemented these principles and lessons have demonstrated repeatedly how effective and powerful they are in achieving tangible and meaning-ful results. It is the success formula for an entrepreneur who chooses the adventure of a lifetime.

Our desire is to share these ideas with you, so that you can apply them to your life and business.

Glossary

Beliefs: Spiritual values that are the essential elements of conviction. They which define your nature, act as guides for behavior, and animate your life and the decisions you make.

Entrepreneur: A person on an adventure who thrives on occupying the space between Spiritual Objective, Mythic Story, the Strategic Vision and the Reality of the business.

Mythic Story: The story that shares the events, courage, and principles upon which the business was created. It is the story that connects all aspects of your business and is the basis for the company's identity. The mythic story is the spirit of all codes of moral and ethical conduct that makes explicit the intention for doing business. It is the pattern of beliefs that gives meaning and structure to the life of the business.

Reality: The measurable processes, procedures and practices of making the business viable, healthy, and profitable in a way that empowers the business to serve the owner(s).

Spiritual Objective: A statement representing your core values and beliefs that make real a sense of the vital principles which give you spiritual significance and meaning.

Strategic Vision: It is the dream that you make into reality. A written narration of how you conceive your business and how it will perform. Once documented, it becomes the benchmark from which all behaviors in the business are guided and directed.

Values: Ideals, qualities, and principles that people consider desirable in and of themselves.

1
The Raven's Story
Planting the Seeds of Good

S mall business is not unlike a thundercloud. Viewed from a distance a storm cloud reaches majestically into the clarity of the sky. It is crystal white at the top, from the sun's rays, full of promise and potential. Black ominous winds churn at the bottom. Rumbling thunder roars, lightning flashes spark and warn of the powerful bedlam beneath its exterior beauty. Inside the regal magnificence of the storm cloud, all hell is breaking loose. It is terrifying!

Like the storm cloud, the same beauty and thunderous chaos is in the universe of small business. In the United States, there are over 15 million companies operating with 1 to 100 employees, growing at about the same rate as the overall economy. Look closely at the inside of a small business and its chaos. Eight percent are brand new every year and 8% go out of business every year.

The common misconception of the small business world is that all this chaos, mayhem, and bedlam, and for some, ultimate failure, is necessary. Small businesses are created and started by a plethora of people. People of all shapes, sizes, races, and creeds, indeed from all corners of life, follow a dream and start a business. They are people who, in their quest to free themselves, begin with an idea to make something better, nurture it, and then launch it into reality. They see a need and act upon it. Knighted with the moniker of entrepreneur, sustained with intense dedication to create a better product or service, they set out to build businesses with enthusiasm and courage. Their creativity and innovation translates into reality, and a business is born to bring it all to market. It is in the hearts, minds, and spirits of these people that ideas are born and put into a formula of doing business. By definition they are entrepreneurs, however, in the end, most are not really entrepreneurs. To become, in the true sense, an entrepreneur and build a successful business, they must accept an adventure of personal exploration. They must accept the adventure to explore the depth of their passion, understand their personal myth and learn to occupy the space between their mythic story and reality. True entrepreneurs are people, who with gallantry and disposition, dig to the deepest reaches of their being to unearth their personal myth and openly share it to the benefit of their business and the people in it. They are open to learning what it is they don't know.

The French gave us the word *entrepreneur*. In English dictionaries, the word is generally accepted to describe a person who undertakes an enterprise or business with the risk of profit or loss. Tracing the word back to its French language origins, however, allows us an insight and understanding of the significance and intention of the word. In French, *entre* means to enter or move between. *Prendre* is a verb meaning to take. The word *preneur* is the noun from *prendre* — meaning a taker. So, following the word back to its origins allows us to define a person who takes the responsibility to move between or to take entry. If we think about the origins of the word in the context of a small business, we observe that an entrepreneur is the person who negotiates the space between the myth (story) of the business and the reality of doing the business. To become an entrepreneur means to be willing to go between—to go between spiritual significance, business myth, and the reality of the business. Occupying the space between the myth and the reality begs the realization that a well-formed myth will translate into an intelligible vision that will in turn drive the reality of the business. It is the myth that creates the reality of the business. By working in-between the myth and reality of a business, the entrepreneur advances the reality of shaping the business into sustainable, ongoing growth and success.

People who think of themselves as undertaking an adventure personify thriving between myth and the reality of a business. Accepting the adventure, indeed fully realizing it, will lead the entrepreneur to freedom and prosperity. This is the *spirit* of the entrepreneur. Entrepreneurs on an adventure recognize, acknowledge, and honor their core beliefs. From their core beliefs they navigate themselves and their business through all challenges and adversity to the Holy Grail of success. Their core beliefs shepherd them, providing focus and comfort, in the knowledge that no matter what the conditions of life, they create their reality. Entrepreneurs on an adventure engage life with enthusiasm. They are energized by the excitement of each new endeavor and subsequently energize the people around them.

By and large, our clients come to us sensing they are standing at a fork in the road with their business, and more importantly, in their life. One fork is the path of the quest, the repetition of routine, which leads to doing things the same way they always have been done. It is a path of recurrence that repeats the experience of frustration and acceptance of the same, often mundane, results.

The other fork is the path of adventure. It leads to doing things differently. It is a path that engages the best people have to offer by using wisdom to transform the business. It gives the owner freedom and abundance to live a full and rich life.

It is all a matter of choice. You decide how you wish to live, think and act out your life. Are you on an adventure — or are you on a quest? It's that simple. Once you have made the decision to be on an adventure or to remain in the bedlam of the quest, you set the course, outcomes, and attitude of your life. You will manifest the reality of your thinking. If you choose the path of adventure, it will create revolutionary change that will set your business apart qualitatively from your competition.

To begin the entrepreneurial adventure, we want to share with you a mythic legend. It comes from the Abenake people who live on the Lorintide plateau, in the Mistasini Forest in northern Canada. It is the story of Raven. We have modified it a little bit just for your benefit.

The Raven was born the son of the Thunderbird. He was born with white feathers. The Thunderbird was sent to the Mother Earth to rid it of all evil and bad things. The Thunderbird would fly around the earth and destroy all that was bad. Like his father, Raven took up the task of ridding the Mother Earth of all evil. He grew into a smart and courageous warrior.

One day, the Raven was flying around the forest and he saw a long house. He had never seen a long house before, so he didn't know if it was good or evil. The Raven flew down to the top of a tree that was near the long house and waited and watched.

The long house spoke to Raven and invited him in through the open door. Being smart and courageous, Raven watched with curiosity but did not move from the tree. The long house again spoke to the Raven and invited him to enter. Raven spread his wings and flew up into the sky and circled the long house. He was still not sure weather the long house was good or evil. Then he flew down to the long house and perched himself on the peak above the door. The long house spoke again, "Raven, come into me. It is warm in here and you will be comfortable."

The Raven just sat on the peak of the long house wondering what to do. The long house spoke to the Raven for the fourth time and invited him in. Raven jumped off the peak of the house and with all of his courage flew through the door into the long house.

Inside the long house Raven found a fire in the very center. It was a good fire. It was the fire of life. As Raven approached the fire it began to pulse with his heartbeat.

The fire spoke to the Raven and told him the four great lessons of life.

The fire spoke the first lesson. "You are the Mystery and the Mystery is you. You cannot change this and if you think of yourself as separate you will have a hard life full of sickness, difficulty, and disease."

Then the fire of life told Raven the second great lesson of life. The fire said, "All things are Sacred. They are sacred because they are created by the Great Mystery."

As Raven watched the fire, it started to get bigger and told the third lesson. "Respect and maintain the differences."

The fire got bigger again and spoke the fourth and last lesson: "Remember, only the earth and sky last forever, make every day a good day to die."

The fire of life got even bigger and reached up to embrace the raven. When the embrace ended, the Raven's feathers had been singed black. Next to the Raven's feet was a small medicine bag. It was a gift from the fire. The fire of life spoke to the Raven and said, "Inside the medicine bag are the seeds of good. Plant the seeds of good in your life and they will grow like strawberries. Then there will be no room for evil or bad things in your life or on the Mother Earth."

Your business is a vehicle to serve your life by planting the seeds of good.

Chapter Summary
Key Points:

• Owning a small business doesn't have to mean chaos, mayhem, bedlam, and loss.

• Failure doesn't have to mean going out of business. Failure simply means not orchestrating the business to serve your life.

• A true entrepreneur must accept an adventure of personal exploration.

• Creating the spirit of the entrepreneurial adventure involves four basic systems:
   1. Understand the vital principles of your spiritual significance. We call it your Spiritual Objective and discuss it in detail in Chapter 3.
   2. Explore and share your business myth. We call it your Mythic Story. It is the spirit in all codes of moral and ethical conduct that form the foundation for doing business. The seven elements for creating your myth are contained in Chapter 4.
   3. Document your dream along with clear goals and objectives. This is the foundation from which to build a successful business. It invites people to align with the business and it benefits both you and those who join the company. We call it your Strategic Vision and coach you through this process in Chapter 5.
   4. Occupying the space between your myth and reality. This is a key characteristic of truly becoming a successful entrepreneur. We discuss ways to do this throughout the book and how to celebrate your success each step of the journey in Chapter 6.

Questions:

1. What are the apprehensions that are keeping you from living your dream?
2. Are you perfectly clear about what you want from your business?
3. What space do you now occupy most of the time in your business?
4. How do you consistently know if your business is on the right track?

Notes for the Spirit of my Adventure:

2
The Four Lessons

There are many gifts of wisdom embedded in the Raven's story. It is a story of transformation. The raven was born the son of the Thunderbird, white as the driven snow. The Thunderbird deity originated with the Native Americans of North America to give meaning to the chaos of the tremendous rainstorms that roamed the vast prairies. They perceived the weather to be in conflict with baneful powers resident on the Earth Mother. It was believed that the Great Mystery sent Thunderbird, with lightning in its eyes and the rush of its wings, to make wind and thunder to vanquish the destructive powers with rain to purify the earth. To the people of the plains, the appearance of the Thunderbird heralded the regeneration of life.

Like the Thunderbird, the Raven takes up his father's work, ridding the Mistasini Forest of destructive powers inhabitant in the woodland. While doing the task of his legacy, Raven happens upon the long house. The long house is unfamiliar to the Raven's experience and causes the story's hero to pause cautiously and reflect. The long house calls the Raven to enter. Yet Raven is unsure of the dangers. He only allows himself to move closer tentatively, ever cautious of potential dangers. Finally, after the fourth summons, Raven abandons all trepidation. With courage and leaving cunning aside, Raven leaps from his perch and dares to enter the lodge of the Fire of Life. Warmed by the wisdom of the fire, Raven is given four significant and critical lessons as a gift from the Great Mystery. After the lessons are taught, the fire embraces the Raven and he is transformed. The Raven is no longer white as the driven snow but singed black as we know him today. This transformation signals that once the wisdom of the lessons is realized, the Raven cannot be the same. The final gesture of grace is the gift of the medicine bag filled with the seeds of good. Like the Raven, for business owners to be successful and to live a meaningful and purposeful life, they must transform, from the manager, technician or inventor to an entrepreneur. They must go on an adventure, learn The Four Lessons and use this wisdom to transform their company. Then they must take themselves to the space between their Spiritual Objective and Mythical Story and their Strategic Vision that drives the reality of making the business work to serve their life. It is from this space that the entrepreneur plants the seeds of good.

From our years of coaching people just like you, in businesses just like yours, we have learned the formula of transformation for becoming an entrepreneur on an adventure. As such, we take the lessons given to the Raven and translate them into the language of business for you.

From our experience, we plant the seeds of good.

The Entrepreneurial Adventure

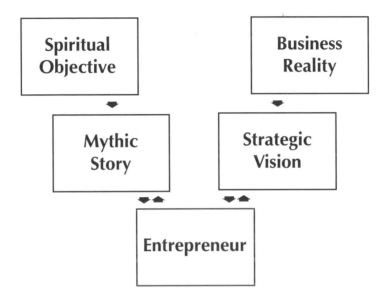

LESSON 1:
You are the mystery and the mystery is you.

What we know is that life is a mystery. However, you personally define this spiritual mystery— God, Yahweh, Creator, Buddha, Great Spirit or Zen— you are an integral part of it. The modern day movie Star Wars claims it as the force. This force, this mystery, is universally recognized in all human cultures and throughout all human activities, however subtle or obvious. It is a force, omnipresent in the universe, with which all of us will eventually reconcile. Regardless of how you claim this mystery, or how you outwardly express your spiritual nature, realize completely that you are actively participating in the harmonic dance of this mystery. It is a dance that you cannot shun. You have no choice in the matter.

It is impossible by any Herculean effort, to separate your "Self" from this mystery. Any efforts you make to define your "Self" as apart from the shared being of the universal truths of the mystery will ultimately end in emotional bankruptcy and failure. To sustain an illusion of separateness takes a lot of emotional energy, which only results in disease, frustration, despair, and a likelihood of an early death. Pretending we are not connected to each other, to the Earth around us, and to the Mystery leads to excessive behaviors: anger, substance abuse, and a variety of psychological disorders. To preserve separateness takes conscious and physical work and only serves to feed the ego that which it wants. It sets impregnable boundaries around your being that close down your capacity to love and share. We may make many efforts to distinguish ourselves as above and apart from others and the Mystery. In the end, however, we are just lonely. It is exhausting, with no return on the effort. This effort of will redirects one's personal energy from the embedded truth that life is a mystery. So why bother?

Realization of your shared being with the "Mystery" will free you from the desperation of separateness and fragmentation. Let it flow. Give yourself permission to drop the pretense of being separate. Become one with the Mystery. Free your ego and all its subsequent needs from the demands of separation. Embrace and become one with your mystery. Allow yourself to broaden your world-view. Permit your intuition to keep you alert to the powerful and multiple possibilities nested within the mystery waiting just for you. By doing so, creativity becomes natural, integral, unencumbered, and fun. Health and well being become habitual and sustainable. Possibilities and opportunities will abound without a need to control.

You can think about and discuss anything, then choose the right thing to do. Prosperity flows, as your myth translates to a tangible, energetic reality. Accepting your inseparable connection to your mystery, frees you to make decisions that positively affect all aspects of your life and those that you love and influence.

Applying the wisdom, "You are the mystery and the mystery is you," into your business is to say: you are the business and the business is you. You can not separate your "Self" from it. Stated more accurately, the business is a reflection of you. You are the spirit of your business. The business will reflect your actions and attitudes. As you are so is the business. If you find your business struggling, it is because you are struggling. If you find your business is not growing it is because you are not growing. You cannot separate your "spirit" from the actions, attitudes, and events in the business.

Choose to be on an adventure. Let the business express your inner goodness and willingness to seek the Holy Grail of success. It is contagious. The success of your life and the business is within your being. Explore the reflection of the business and search its meaning. Listen to the subtleties of the business rhythm and tune your behavior to maximize bringing your vision into reality. Allow your business to serve your life, others, and your Mystery.

Once you make the choice to be on an adventure, you position yourself with capacity to work on the business, not in it. Decide that you truly want to understand your integral connection with the Mystery and achieve what you desire. Make this decision seriously. It will require acceptance and attention. Be mindful, the process is about enjoying each moment as you learn to "get out of your own way." Affirm your relationship to the mystery and let your life, and business, flow.

The business is always a reflection of you.

LESSON 2:
All things are sacred.

All things are sacred because they have their source within the Mystery. It means exactly what it says— all things are sacred. The trees, rocks, rivers, lakes, and all the creatures living within the environment are sacred. All the creative expression of human kind is sacred. All which begins in the Mystery and manifests in reality is sacred. Accepting this concept creates a philosophical paradigm that expands our awareness and connection with the Mystery. We can marvel at the beauty of the world around us. We are freed from the notion of possession and open to creativity and abundance. If we can't give a possession away, then it possesses us. If we evade the notion of possession, with all its encumbrances, and affirm ourselves as caretakers of our material wealth, we will not be adversely affected when they move away from us. Indeed, we can deliberately move the collected abundance when we no longer have an attachment to or need for it. Moving acquisitions we no longer use out of our life and to someone else is to participate in the great flow of life. Let another put to use what you don't need or want. Make room in your life for what you can use to its fullest potential. Rid yourself of the rest.

In the context of business, this lesson has extra-ordinary potential. Everything you do is important (sacred). It follows, only do what is important to make your life and business thrive. Be deliberate and focused in all that you do. As the business owner, know that your accountability is limited to two key elements, vision and capital. Concentrate on your behavior, thinking, and actions around only these responsibilities with precision. Free yourself from the rest. In a like manner, free your employees to do what they do best within the context of their responsibility. Coach them to only do what is important (sacred) within the context of their responsibility and position results. Rid yourself and your business of all unnecessary, unimportant, and labor intensive tasks and chores that do not serve the Strategic Vision of your company. Observe the people and processes within the business. If people in your company tell you they are busy, ask them what they are busy doing. Confirm that it is sacred and that it supports your Strategic Vision.

To become an entrepreneur you must take yourself between. Be the person willing to go between your myth and the reality of the business, so that you thrive and prosper. Fully accepting the wisdom of this lesson will take you beyond the temporal attributes of competence and skill. It is a wisdom that requires you to consent to spiritual growth. It will define your approach to life as a sacred work, living creatively as opposed to reactively. You will become the link between your Spiritual Objective, Mythic Story, and the Strategic Vision that inspires the people who drive the business Reality. Be open to opportunities that move in harmony with your myth. When this lesson becomes a discipline you will continually refine and cultivate only that which is sacred. It will also help you to see current reality more clearly.

Only do what is important.

LESSON 3:
Respect and maintain the differences.

L earning to respect and maintain the differences is a boost to self-esteem. Maintaining and respecting differences frees us from the responsibility to direct or control the lives of others. Living with this lesson allows you to escape being responsible for the behavior, state of well being, or status of another person. You can respect a person for having a philosophy, point of view, or a political stance, without being compelled to accept or agree with them. After carefully listening, we make the right decisions that manifest the highest potential of our purpose. Likewise, when appropriate, you can share your philosophy and coach with sage advice. Respecting and maintaining the differences positions you to learn, allows you to be intrigued and confirm a meaningful life. You become responsible for only your decisions and actions.

By practicing this kind of thinking, you can allow people to define themselves without prejudice. This is to say, that if a person is conservative politically, or a staunch feminist, a homemaker, or business person, you can learn and explore that persons view of the world, no matter how consistent or contradictory to your own, and be secure with your own life, definitions, and boundaries. You are not responsible for changing them, nor do they have any responsibility to change you. Respecting and maintaining the differences can enrich your life through the exploration of other people's paradigms. In the final analysis, you can make the choice to change your thinking by respecting another's ideas or authenticate your differences by choosing to maintain them.

Subsequently, your self-esteem will be strengthened. You will avoid the blemish of guilt and minimize frustration. Any responsibilities for the behavior of others are eliminated, and your life is streamlined.

The richness of this lesson can be translated quite literally into the context of your business. Respect is a basic human attribute and the expectation of it as a virtue of your company will go a long way in establishing the foundation for long-term growth and success. Maintaining the differences allows you and your employees to appreciate the demands of the various, and sometimes conflicting, positions and points of view within the business. Respecting and maintaining differences builds cooperation through the management structure by holding people accountable to a standard, while allowing them to succeed and support the character of your company. Make it incumbent on everyone in your business to willingly understand the needs, demands, and responsibilities of others.

The only thing you control is your vision.

LESSON 4:
Only the earth and sky last forever,
make every day a good day to die.

Every day of your life counts. Live it to its fullest potential. "Be your own self, at your very best, all the time," was the advice of William H. Danforth, founder of Ralston Purina. It is a tall order, especially when you consider the imperative of "all the time." Our admonition is to live your life to its full measure. Do only the things that truly matter to you, your family, community, and business. Outwardly demonstrate that you care and openly encourage what is possible.

When all is said and done at the end of the day, when you put your head on your pillow, ask yourself: "Was this a good day to die?" Ask yourself: "Have you put your very best forward?" Have you taken the steps, exercised the responsibilities, delivered on your promises, and focused your efforts on living your Spiritual Objective? If you have, rejoice and celebrate. Give yourself a hug. If you haven't, or feel you could have done better, ready yourself for the next day.

With a clear Spiritual Objective, a Myth well defined, and the Strategic Vision of your business explicit comes the task to define the reality that makes your life and business work for you. People and process are the components of strategy that collaborate and drive your business to manifest your Strategic Vision. As the business owner, you become the entrepreneur, providing vision and capital, working between the Myth and the Reality of your adventure. Be the best, all the time. Make every day a good day to die. Settle for nothing less.

My own self, at my very best, all the time
William H. Danforth

And so we begin the adventure of how to make the transformation and become an entrepreneur. As you choose this adventure you will leave behind the manager, technician, or inventor in you to become an entrepreneur, to dare to go between your myth and reality. You will learn to dance in the mystery and utilize your entrepreneurial intelligence to its greatest potential. It is a process of discovery, change, and learning that is required to make the adaptations which will allow you to create a successful fulfilling business. We will share with you how to exercise the wisdom of your Myth, clarify your Spiritual Objective, and create the Reality of your business. You will rise above the storm, free yourself from the daily chaos, and move to a place where the business serves your life and the lives of your employees. It all begins with exploring the essence of your spirit, becoming cognizant of your myth, defining your Spiritual Objective, and then taking the right action in the reality of allowing business to prosper and grow. And in the process, grow yourself.

Let the adventure begin.

Chapter Summary
Key Points

• Commit to learn what it is that you don't know to transform into the entrepreneur you want to become.
• Accept the challenge to learn how to occupy the space between myth and reality.
• Infuse your newly found wisdom into your business so it serves your life.
• Translate the Four Lessons given to Raven into your business.

Lesson 1: The business is always a reflection of you.
Lesson 2: Only do what is important.
Lesson 3: The only thing you control is your vision.
Lesson 4: Be your own self, at your very best, all the time.

Questions:

1. How is your business a reflection of you?
2. What did you do today that was really not important?
3. Are you in control of how you spend your time?
4. How did you plant the seeds of good today?

Notes for the Spirit of my Adventure:

3
The Entrepreneurial Adventure
You are the Mystery and the Mystery is You

In the beginning is the hero: the entrepreneurial hero. The Mystery is revealed in the entrepreneurial legend. At first glance, the legend appears to suggest that an entrepreneur starts a new business or enterprise. We know this to be untrue. We understand clearly from our client base that inventors, managers, and technicians are the people who start new businesses. They are people who have reached within themselves, found what they want, assessed their personal resources, taken the risk, and stepped out of normal life pathways to bring a new product or service to market. Armed with courage, ambition, confidence, and ability, they take a great leap of faith. The challenges are met forthright by the entrepreneur, and a business is born. They become business owners; working desperately within the organization to achieve success, often taking responsibility for every detail. They become so busy doing, that they lose sight of what's really important.

A false and misguided myth lurks in the common story of the entrepreneurial hero. Beware. It goes like this.

One day, emerging from the oppression of a dull,

meaningless work-a-day life, the manager, technician or inventor is suddenly inspired with an idea for a new product or service. It is a great idea. With careful planning, the idea is fully realized and made operational. Hope springs eternal that his or her life will dramatically change for the better. The new business will positively impact the world and lead to the Holy Grail of freedom — freedom from a tyrannical boss or the ugly politics of corporate business and the drudgery of a life unfulfilled. The hero is born: a business owner.

The new business owner is the hero of the legend — a hero that sets upon the quest of creating the new product or service and the development of the company that will deliver it. The hero bravely charges into a seemingly insurmountable task, slaying mythical monsters of defeat with the sword of creativity. Smashing the barriers to the goal with a mallet of intellect. Scaling the cliffs of adversity with agility supported by the ropes, cleats, and pitons of commitment, ideology, and business acumen. The doors of the business are thrown open to waiting customers. The owner becomes free to enjoy the bounty of riches pouring forth from the new company, live a productive life, and retire in a wealth of happiness with prosperity, able to pursue any desire.

What glorious tales we spin. How wonderful if it were true. Unfortunately, it is a legend fraught with dangerous illusions and filled with unforeseen potential for disaster if we accept it as truth. Michael E. Gerber advises, "The legend reeks of nobility, of lofty, extra-human efforts, of a prodigious commitment to larger-than-life ideals."[1] It is an illusion and a myth that "finds its roots in this country in a romantic belief that small businesses are started by entrepreneurs, when in fact most are not." It is a barren legend, but it doesn't have to be that way.

At the moment the business is born, the owner has chosen a path that must lead to a transformation from the inventor, manager, or technician to an entrepreneur for the business to survive. It is an adventure. And it is here that we want to inspire you, to excite you, to kindle the spirit of learning for your entrepreneurial adventure. We will share stories of the many heroes we have coached to create a balanced life of freedom, wealth, and happiness.

Dan Robertson, of Robertson Industries shares his story of becoming a business owner and then discovering the virtues of the entrepreneurial adventure. It is a powerful story of transformation. It is a story of a business owner coached to "take" himself "between" and create a balanced life.

I remember it as if it happened yesterday. I was sitting in my office doing the books for my company. As usual for me it was very late, the office was dark and quiet with the exception of the light in my office and the clack of the calculator. I was struggling with how to make the payroll, pay the vendors, balance the bank account and somehow find the time to visit my family. The word "visit" was so accurate. Since the beginning, when I started my business, I had been doing nothing but working. I had forsaken my family and friends. I justified all of this because I had a great idea. It had a market, and I, you know, just me, could pull it off and find my riches. I thought to myself when I began this business, with a few months of concentrated effort, maybe even a year, the business would be up on its feet and I would have all the free time in the world and the profits would bring me new found riches. That was five years ago. Here I am, all my employees had gone home, still doing the books after 9:00 p.m., having fed on yet another fast food dinner, two hours to go, wondering if my spouse will be awake when I get home.

The radio was on, tuned to the local talk radio station broadcasting a talk show on why small businesses don't work and what to do about it. The person being interviewed was talking about how to manage an entrepreneurial business. The voice was talking to me. This guy knew me! I stopped my work to listen to his enthusiastic coaching. It sounded good, too good to be true. Nonetheless, his stories pegged me, the entrepreneur, trapped in the business. His words made sense, so I called into the show to ask a question, that of course I thought was unique to just me.

The very next day, being inspired by what I had heard on the radio, I called and connected with Jeff, the founder of Thunderlight Resources, who turned out to be the same person interviewed on the talk show. My plan was to interrogate Jeff and discover what his company could do for me. I knew I was ready for change. I simply did not know where to start. I was on the edge. I needed to be safe. I needed to know that it would work.

To my surprise, Jeff turned my interrogation on me. He asked me a lot of questions. They *were not questions about my business, but questions about my life. He wanted to know about how much pain I had endured, and was I truly committed to change. I listened to what he had to say and decided that I would apply his company's coaching system to my business.*

Now, five years later, the strategic work we did with Thunderlight provided the foundation for change that transformed the company and the people in it from a condition of chaos to a condition of order, excitement, and continuous growth.

Today, as CEO of my company, I am only accountable to provide vision and capital toward the attainment of our strategic objective. The profits in my business are 12 times the annual profit when I first heard that radio interview.

What is consistent with this entrepreneurial legend? What are the illusions and where is the reality? Why do business owners fail? Or worse yet, if the business gets underway, why does the owner get stuck "in" the business?

How is it that the hero gets overwhelmed by the volume of work? How is he seduced into an untenable situation, unable to make the business grow, drowning in the day to day task of working the business? How is it the owner/hero becomes alienated from family, friends, faith, and community? Is it because of lack of ability? Not usually. Is it because of a lack of courage, intellect, and willingness to succeed? We don't think so. Is it because of the lack of business skill? Rarely. So what is it that determines entrepreneurial success?

The answer to these questions is simple. *The owner must learn to become an entrepreneur.*

It is here that we want to again inspire you once more to light the fire of your learning spirit and stimulate learning in your business. Peter Senge, in his book *The Fifth Discipline* speaks to the spirit of a learning organization. "Organizations learn only through individuals who learn. Individual learning does not guarantee organizational learning. But without it no organizational learning occurs."[2]

So learn to become an entrepreneur. Rise above the processes and intricacies of doing your business. Launch your entrepreneurial adventure. Position yourself so that the business serves your life and your Spiritual Objective.

Precisely articulating your Spiritual Objective is the first step to truly becoming an entrepreneur. Understanding your Spiritual Objective connects you with your mystery. A Spiritual Objective is a simple summary statement of your core values and beliefs that represents who you are, what you want to be in your world, and validates your spiritual significance and meaning. Revealing your Spiritual Objective is the first step that will launch you into the entrepreneurial adventure.

Discovering Your Spiritual Objective

You are the Mystery and the Mystery is you, and you connect to your mystery by exploring, defining and writing your Spiritual Objective. To begin the entrepreneurial adventure you must first be willing to explore your inner soul, to discover your true purpose, your essential character, your vision of who you are, and to answer the question, "What are you about?"

Our experience of coaching successful business owners to first become entrepreneurs, then to create a dynamic business starts with the creation of their Spiritual Objective. The process requires you to explore your inner self, to discover your most meaningful, spiritual values. Your spiritual values are the essential elements, which you know in your heart, define your nature, guide, and animate your life and the decisions you make. This process requires your full attention so that the documentation that follows becomes a statement of your spiritual beliefs.

The Spiritual Objective is profoundly personal. Discovering your Spiritual Objective obligates you to reach deep into yourself to ascertain and define your essential and basic truths. These truths are the small number of stars in your belief constellation by which you navigate and guide your conduct and behavior. This constellation of beliefs motivates and shepherds the actions of your life journey and the entrepreneurial adventure. A Spiritual Objective will define your leadership and drive your ethics, commitment, and action. You will know you have discovered your Spiritual Objective when you become energized. Your emotions will leap with enthusiasm and excitement about who you truly are.

When exploring for your Spiritual Objective, consider it in two parts: 1) Spiritual: your being, essence, a claim of who you are. 2) Objective: your direction, your aim and purpose, what you desire to achieve. Bringing your Spiritual Objective into awareness is to create a conscious discipline integrated into your daily life. It will become the foundation, firmly established, for the leadership of your business.

You are the mystery and the mystery is you. You are the business and the business is a reflection of you. With a well-formed understanding of your Spiritual Objective, you have taken the first step to becoming an entrepreneur. You are the distinguished identity who establishes and sanctifies the vision, ethics, and moral nature of the business. As you are, so will your business be. As you create your business or change the business, realize that your stories and values become the myth that will sustain your endeavors.

Welcome to the adventure.

Example Statements of Spiritual Objectives

• *To serve humanity through my creative skills while sharing love, peace and joy through feelings and intimacy.*

• *To illuminate my spirit and share its love in a way that creates a kinder, healthier, safer and more prosperous world.*

• *To honor and glorify God in all that I do so that my life will reflect His love for me.*

• *Enjoy life, rich with love, full of challenge, leading others to be their best.*

Chapter Summary
Key Points

• You are the mystery and the mystery is you.
• Create a balanced life of abundance.
• Be open to learning what you don't know.
• Learn how to create a business that serves your life.
• Learning in the spirit of what needs to be done, not how to do it, produces results.
• Begin by discovering your Spiritual Objective.
• Integrate your core beliefs into your leadership style.
• Be your own self, at your very best, all the time.
• Become an entrepreneur; leave behind the manager, technician, or inventor in you.
• Learn how to transform wisdom into your business.

Questions

Fill in the blanks:

    a. I am a _____ person

    b. I stand for _____

    c. I offer or contribute _____

    d. I receive _____

NOTES 1 Michael E. Gerber, *The E-Myth Revisited*, page 9
       2 Peter Senge, *The Learning Organization*, p148

Notes for the Spirit of my Adventure:

4
Mythic Story
All Things are Sacred

All things are sacred. And so all the things you do in your business should sanctify your Spiritual Objective and affirm your Myth. Your myth, the legend of your business, is the story that shares the events that happened on your epic pursuit to create the company. It shares an explanation of the purpose and reason behind your dream. The myth is the sinew that explains the events that hold the past, present and future together. It is the story that will bind your company together and is the basis for the identity of your business. It is the core ingredient in all codes of moral and ethical conduct and establishes the rules for doing business. It is an outward expression of your core beliefs that gives meaning to the life of the organization. The myth, your story, is sacred. The most sacred thing you can do is to share it.

After the wisdom of your Spiritual Objective is revealed, the next step in the entrepreneurial adventure is creating and understanding your myth. To do so requires an understanding of the elements of a myth and to carefully construct them in a story that describes your journey into the unknown territory of creating a business. It is a hero's myth in which you are the hero.

An exploration of the structure and origins of heroic mythology from the Far East, Asia, Europe, to Africa and the Americas, discloses parallel and common threads woven into the fabric of all myths, regardless of their origin. All hero myths describe a call to adventure and initiation. The myths describe change, make ritual explicit, and affirm the continuity of culture. The lessons, embedded in mythical stories, advise the listener (reader) of the fascinating ways that realities reveal the essence of life.

Hero myths also address the duality of life. The Yin and Yang of the Chinese philosophers, the Egyptian myths of Isis and Osiris, and the Sun and Moon stories of Native America, all disclose the omnipresent duality inherent in life. Often thematic in these myths is the duality of the dynamic tension of the hero's inner self and the reality of the hero's outer life. The mythical stories share the wisdom of this duality, making explicit that the spirit of the adventure manifests in right action in reality. They are deeds born of the hero's core values and from which are created the reality of the outer world. By choosing to go on an adventure, the hero accepts the challenge to explore and define his or her inward spiritual values, then express them outwardly into the world of reality. Thomas Moore calls it the search for The Soul's Code. You might think of it as one's true calling, one's purpose in the world. Peter Senge calls it personal mastery. "It means approaching ones life as a creative work, living life from a creative as opposed to a reactive viewpoint."[3] This exploration is the underlying theme of the myth.

Elements of Myth

Myth has been guiding the behavior of humankind since our earliest beginnings. The first recorded myth, over 6000 years old, is the story of Gilgamesh and Enkidu, a Sumerian tale of best friends conquering a monster together. In the myths told by indigenous peoples the world over, and in the modern big screen myths of today, we find common themes. These themes are rich, proclaiming the common heritage of humankind. These stories define the meaning of our existence and express our hope for the eternal. Joseph Campbell said, "Myths are the stories of our search through the ages, for truth, meaning, and significance. We all need to tell our story to understand our story. We need for life to signify, to touch the eternal, to understand the mysterious, to find out who we are."[4] It is the process of finding out "who" we are, the origin of our myth, that allows us to create and manifest the reality of our existence, be it business, family, or community. Then we find a way to be that person.

J. F. Bierlein, in his book *Parallel Myths* shares with us these notions about myth.

• Myth is constant among all human beings in all times. The patterns, stories, even details contained in myth are found everywhere and among everyone. This is because myth is a shared heritage of ancestral memories, related consciously from generation to generation. Myth may even be part of the structure of our unconscious mind, possibly encoded in our genes.

• Myth is telling of events that happened before written history and of a sense of what is to come. Myth is the thread that holds past, present and future together.

• Myth is a unique use of language that describes

45

the realities beyond our five senses. It fills the gap between the images of the unconscious and the language of conscious logic.

• Myth is the "glue" that holds societies together; it is the basis of identity for communities, tribes, and nations.

• Myth is an essential ingredient in all codes of moral conduct. The rules for living have always derived their legitimacy from their origins in myth and religion.

• Myth is a pattern of beliefs that give meaning to life. Myth enables individuals and societies to adapt to their respective environments with dignity and value. [5]

With this knowledge we can draw forth and define a true heroic entrepreneurial myth. The mythical story you create will be constant throughout your business for all of time, hold the past, present, and future together, describe the realities of the business, hold the culture together, define the moral basis of conduct, and give dignity, value, and alignment to your employees. It is a myth similar to the legend of Parsifal, the Arthurian knight who sought the Holy Grail, enduring challenges and adventure, only to find that he held the goal in himself all along. It could be like the Norse legend of Brynhilde, who created the world of mortals by conquering the corrupt gods. Your myth may be similar to the Navajo story of the Spider Woman, who creates the world and explains the ways to live in it. Regardless, it is the myth of a hero. It is the mythical story of a champion, who, with courage, accepts the call to adventure, has the fortitude to be different, the determination to define himself, and make changes that positively impact his life and the world around him or her.

Embedded in every myth is an ethos, a moral statement that establishes the guiding beliefs of a person, culture or institution. Close examination of Jeff's personal myth demonstrates the successful development of these Mythic Story characteristics.

*O*n *the northern shores of Lake Michigan sits Miniwanca (land of many waters), a 200-acre summer camp, founded more than seventy-five years ago by four men including the father of Ralston Purina, William Danforth.*

From all the summers I spent there growing up, what has stayed with me the most is the introduction at age twelve to a Four-Fold way of life combining the mental, physical, social, and spiritual aspects we all encompass.

People seek the freedom to discover who they really are, then desire the flexibility to find the place to be that person. It was after my father's death that I realized I had a choice to find the place to be me, so I returned to Miniwanca. For 25 years prior to that moment of recognition I was taking care of everyone except myself. And thought I had it all under control.

Fortunately, major life events can be wake-up calls to change unhealthy patterns and provide the platform for change. It was during these summers that I became intrigued by the notion you could orchestrate your business to serve your life. With this clarity began a transition from a fifteen year business career that was consuming my life to one of serving mankind through my creative skills while making an impact on the world by sharing the abundant elements of love, peace and joy.

I had remained rooted in the status quo, the

comfortable path, the one I knew until dad died. That event had the impetus I needed to take the road less traveled. I began tearing down everything that was faulty, right to the foundation. As I was rebuilding, there were no coincidences. I met exactly the people I was supposed to, all explaining their perspective and way of thinking about business and life and the interrelationship between the two.

With this perspective came tools and the formation of Thunderlight Resources, a company whose foundation provides resources for others to take life's journey with a guide. A systematic, step-by-step approach to help people discover who they really are, and then orchestrate their life around what they want. Thunderlight coaches business owners on the spirit of the entrepreneurial adventure.

M yths come in many shapes and sizes. By their nature, myths construct a framework around themes of tragedy, redemption, transformation, comedy, creation and heroic deeds. "Fables, fairy tales, literature, epics, tales told around campfires, and the scriptures of great religions are all packages of myth that transcend time, place and culture."[6] Myths define our commonality, establish our values, sustain our cultures, and illuminate the rich diversity of our humanity across the barriers of time and history. Likewise in your business, a well-formed mythology will sustain your Strategic Vision and the reality of forging a business that works.

Writing Your Myth

U pon completion of the development and documentation of your Spiritual Objective, the next step is to begin writing your Mythic Story. The myth is an expression of yourself and your spiritual objective as it relates to your company. It is the story that expresses your commitment, meaning, and significance as applied to the business and your life. It will be the story you share with employees, vendors, clients, customers, family and friends. Your Mythic Story already exists. The task is to document it so that it can be shared with consistency. Once documented and shared, the Mythic Story will set the tone of your business and govern the working environment and the core values from which those that participate in the business will believe, operate and perform. The story should clearly demonstrate the ethics, behavior, expectations, and focus for which you stand. Be mindful of the intention of your myth, as it will be repeated. It puts people in touch with the spirit of you and your company.

Creating your myth is a straightforward and deliberate process. Reveal your myth with deliberation and intention. It is a practice ever-present for successful businesses large and small. Think of any large company and you will find the hero's myth embedded somewhere in their lore. IBM, Proctor and Gamble, Deluxe Corporation, Starbucks, Dell Computer, Disney — all have a Mythic Story. These stories make explicit the history of the person that started the business and include the original vision of the founder. In the stories are the guiding principles and core values of the business, established in the beginning by the founder, the entrepreneurial hero.

As you begin writing your Mythic Story, think about yourself in relationship to your business endeavor. Be aware that you are setting the standards and principles that will create history, make clear your core values, and navigate the company. A well-written Mythic Story will constitute the endurance that holds your company together through the best and worst of times. It is the spirit of your Mythic Story that will endow the organization and the generations that follow.

The Mythic Story is about you, your aspirations, spiritual objective, and core values. It is about how all of these issues influence the experience of your enterprise. As you begin the process of writing, consider the seven basic components of myth. Thinking through each component will help you recall important aspects of your history to share. These components will guide you and assist you to determine the distinguishing characteristics of your Mythic Story. This list has no particular order or taxonomy. Let your story emerge from your inner self and write it as it comes to you. Take your time and strive for excellence in its readability and simplicity.

Seven Components for creating your Myth

- Declaration of Spirit
- The Call to Adventure
- Creating the Environment
- Formula for Success
- Slaying the Dragons
- Core Values
- The Experience of Transformation

Declaration of Spirit

In the myth of Parsifal we are told the story of a young man, protected in his youth by his mother from all the evils of life, who sets forth on a quest to discover himself and the meaning of his life and to fulfill his potential. At the beginning of the myth, Parsifal declares he will be a Knight and seek the Holy Grail. He is on an outward quest for the Holy Grail, which ultimately he discovers, is in his own spirit and soul. Thematic throughout the myth is Parsifal's unrelenting commitment to the spirit of his adventure, his call to find the Holy Grail. An entrepreneur is not unlike Parsifal in his pursuit of the Holy Grail of success and fulfillment. What differentiates an entrepreneur from Parsifal is the advantage and advanced knowledge that the Holy Grail we seek is in the spirit of the business. It is the spirit of the business that will ultimately determine the boundaries of its success.

A declaration of spirit in your Mythic Story is a statement about the spirit of the business. Declare the spirit in a manner that will bring clarity to your vision of the company. Be mindful that the spirit of the business you establish will always exist, past, present and future. The spirit of your company is the benchmark that will guide the enthusiasm of the employees. It is the cornerstone by which the processes within the organization are developed and executed. The spirit of the company propels the right action for doing business. This statement of "spirit" makes clear the vitality, energy, fortitude and nature of the business. It is a statement intended to be constant. It is to be lived fully by all those who participate in doing the day to day activities, planning, and development of the enterprise. Moreover, it is the quintessential spirit to which all who participate can relate, enthusiastically support, and work to confirm and declare every minute of the day. This spirit statement is about "who we are," and "how we do it."

Eventually, if done well, a declaration of spirit can be condensed and used to create a marketing tag line for your business. One example we can all relate to tags the Avis Company. "We try harder," announced without question the intention of the company. Nike's "Just do it" has sent a clear message for years. Thunderlight Resources uses the tag line, "Tools for the Journey... because it's your life." It's simple, direct and powerful.

The Call to Adventure

Explain in your Mythic Story how you were called to the adventure of creating the business. Share the events that lead to your decision to take the risk of leaving your security and well being. Reveal how you mustered the courage to begin the process of new business. Fill the story with anecdotes, poignant and humorous, that represent this fundamental courage. Let the story reveal how you formed the idea. What were the risks in the beginning? How did you struggle to make it work? Sharing your call to adventure is rich with the substance of the hero's courage. Explain the character of your grit and tenacity. Show how you accepted the challenges of starting the business.

Our friend Ron Behee, President of Network Analysis, Inc., shares his call to adventure in the following Mythic Story.

NAI Company Story

*J*erry Gaski, the author of the SINDA/G thermal analysis software package, was a true genius. He created an elegant piece of software that even today, with all of our programming expertise and technology, we just scratch our heads asking "How did he figure this out 30 years ago?" We are able to expand the software's capabilities, but simply cannot improve its core structure.

As a thermal engineer, I had heard so many good things about this thermal analyzer that I decided to switch from my current software and use it for my future thermal design work. Jerry and his wife Jan came to Arizona to install the software, and took my wife and me out to a fabulous Chinese dinner in Scottsdale. I loved the software so much that I used it exclusively for the next 10 years for all of my thermal analysis. I also enjoyed getting to know Jerry and Jan, who always were available when I needed help.

While Jerry created a timeless piece of software, he and his wife Jan never actively marketed the software. Rather they sold it by word-of-mouth. I was surprised to find out that a typed summary sheet was their only piece of sales literature. In 1995, I took control of the company and started to run it more like a traditional engineering software company. Jerry and Jan had a wonderful, personal friendly touch with their customers, treating them like part of an extended family. I was determined to keep the personal touch that Jerry and Jan had as we grew. To better understand our *customers' needs, I did not want to send non-technical sales people on visits. I went myself or sent one of our experts in the field of thermal analysis. I found most of our customers wanted us to come and visit them, to show them new products, and to discuss their thermal design needs. They would send out meeting notices, and sometimes personally bring coffee, soft drinks, or donuts to the meeting. It was not exactly like trying to get a foot in the door. After one meeting at an aerospace company in Southern California, an engineer walked up to me and said, "This was really a good meeting." I asked him why, and he said, "Because you are a thermal engineer and know where we come from." During the meeting, he obviously saw my knowledge and excitement for our product in solving thermal problems. What he did not see was, as a user, I liked the product so much that I bought the company!*

Creating the Environment

Creating a business is not only about generating success and abundance for the entrepreneur, but also about doing so for the people courageous enough to join you on your adventure. Set the tone for the working environment. Let people in your company know in your Mythic Story you are willing to share the wealth, both emotional and financial, and how you intend to do it. Doing so will develop alignment, trust, and commitment to success far beyond your expectations. An environment of reciprocity establishes the avenue for employees, your most precious asset, to align with the Strategic Vision.

When William R. Hotchkiss started his printing company in 1915 on his chicken farm in Minnesota, he had no idea that the Second World War was looming on the horizon. When the war came, his commitment to employees and country led him to the decision to guarantee employment for any one called to battle upon their return from the war effort. When the wartime economy got into full swing and generating business was difficult, Hotchkiss could not always make the payroll. To compensate his employees, he partially paid them with shares of stock in the fledgling printing company. Ultimately, Hotchkiss created an environment of reciprocal commitment, profound honesty, and service by promising sustained employment and respecting the need for security and stability. Based on commitment to his employees and to his business, despite seemingly insurmountable adversity, W. R. Hotchkiss became the founder of Deluxe Check Printers. His story, his myth, became the endowment of spirit for the company. Told over and over, shared with every new employee on the first day of service, Deluxe Corporation generated 1.6 billion dollars in revenue seventy five years after its beginnings. You can do it. Remember, Hotchkiss began as a small business owner, just like you.

Keep your story above trivial world views. Each person you employ, every vendor, client and customer you do business with will have his or her own world-view. It surfaces in their politics, religion and ethnicity. Your myth is about your company and the way it will go about the day-to-day task of conducting business. Keep the company myth far beyond the limitations of world-views, discrimination, prejudice, politics, religion, gender and ethnicity. Make clear to all who come to participate that they will work in an environment which provides an equal and fair opportunity to succeed within the enterprise.

Formula for Success

In classical myths, the hero is given the formula for success either by experience or the wisdom of a sage. Define in your story the practical ways, expectations, and processes that make the company successful. Let the story reveal the personality of the company. Make apparent and explicit the formula for success. Express your desire and opinions about the ways by which the enterprise will continue to grow, serve, and provide. Make it easy for your employees to know how to be successful. Be explicit. A statement of the success formula defines the attitudes, activities, and methods that support the company and give it continuity. It is a statement about "what we do" and "how we do it," regardless of the products and services of the enterprise.

When our friend Casey Journigan, President and CEO of Arcadia Chair Company wrote his story, there was no doubt about his formula for success.

Arcadia. We make furniture. We sell solutions. Originally, all we did was sell solutions and let others make the furniture. That's back when my father, Wayne, and I were independent manufacturers' reps. We were in business to make sales, which we did by always focusing on the customers needs.

By the time we bought Arcadia Chair Company, our "whatever it takes" mentality had become second nature to us. And we quickly discovered that we were still in the business of selling solutions; we had simply expanded our capability to include manufacturing.

Early on, a customer asked if we could make a particular chair for his standards program. We previously hadn't done much business with this customer, and we didn't yet know what we could and couldn't manufacture. But we did know what the customer needed, so we went to work. Forty-eight hours later, the customer had a sample product to review and ultimately purchased hundreds of that particular chair. We have continued to develop other products to meet their specific requirements, and now, years later, California Federal Bank remains one of Arcadia's most loyal customers. Because they get more than just furniture from us — they get solutions.

Being flexible and responsive to our customers is everybody's top priority at Arcadia. We are a manufacturing company comprised of sales-minded people from the front office to the factory floor. And we are committed to do "whatever it takes" to make it easy for all the customers to do business with Arcadia.

Slaying the Dragons

In mythological stories the hero often embarks on a journey that is full of challenges to his or her capabilities, virtues, and commitment. These are the dragons of the quest. There are dangerous consequences if the hero fails to slay these mythical beasts.

Kathleen Noble, in her book *The Sound of the Silver Horn*, explains the process of creating the modern female myth, and so eloquently describes the mythical journey of the ancient and modern female hero. In this book, she updates the masculine myths of the past to make them meaningful to women. As is often the case, however, Noble's ideas enriched the understanding of the power of myth for both contemporary females and males. For the challenges the entrepreneur will face, male or female, involve balancing one's inner needs with the demands and tasks of the business. In today's world, all heroes must take into account not only their own goals, but also the goals of all of those people in their charge.

"From medieval legends of El Cid and King Arthur to contemporary stories of Batman and Bruce Lee, popular tales portray male heroes as exceptional people who epitomize the greatest attributes and aspirations of men. These archetypal heroes are usually successful warriors who display superior strength and courage, or men who wield social, political, or spiritual power. The hero gives shape to himself, and he lives life on his own terms regardless of cost. Historically, the mythic hero has been revered for his great capacity for life and for pursuing 'higher goals.' In myths, heroes are expected to develop resilience, autonomy, and self-reliance to approach the challenges in their lives with intelligence and creativity, and to act with integrity in all endeavors. Their quest challenges them to roam the inner or outer worlds in search of new knowledge and to use that knowledge to serve their fellow creatures. He who seeks the Grail, the mysterious core of each mythic journey, is the quintessential hero, even if he perishes in the process." [7]

Embed in your Mythic Story clear expectations of

how the people and the business are expected to behave with dignity. Establish how people should conduct themselves in normal day-to-day operations, as well as in a crisis. Write about employees whose actions and behavior exemplified the spirit of the business and how they accomplished it. Share your expectations of conduct and performance so that people have a consistent understanding of what behavior is anticipated, regardless of the events or issues at hand.

Be clear about how you deal with conflict, for you know it will surely come. Starting a business is no easy task. The road to success is often fraught with challenges that strain financial and human resources. Be honest and let the story include the ups and downs of the venture. Share the frustrations, anxiety, disappointments, and the will you have to overcome adversity to assure the success of the business.

Core Values

Illuminate the core values of the organization in plain talk. Think about the values of your Spiritual Objective. You are the leader, and as you do, so will your employees. Make distinct your position on commitment, honesty, and integrity, as well as your expectations for employees, vendors, clients and customers to understand and align with them. Leave no room for any misunderstanding of your values. The core values are the constructs, girders, posts, and beams that give structure to the organization. Clear values, core to the business, set the parameters for decisions that make the enterprise work with grace and elegance. Explain the core values of your business in the story you write. Make them clear, concise, and evident. The owners of Arcadia Chair Company proudly display their core values throughout their corporate office and manufacturing plants.

Arcadia Core Values

Attitudes
Positive and Energetic

Employees
Think More Highly of Others than Themselves (sic)

Enlightenment
Fully Express Life in Healthy and Caring Atmosphere

Customer Relationships
Developed Through Personalized Attention and Service

Customers
Know They Are Highly Valued and Appreciated

Environment
Creative, Innovative, Teamwork Oriented

Recognized For
Honesty, Reliability, and Responsiveness

The Experience of Transformation

Of all the businesses we know, eventually every company finds itself challenged to the point of renewal. It may be an unexpected down turn in the financial picture, or a completely unexpected order for product and service that is beyond the immediate capacity of the company to deliver. Or on a more personal level, it could be the death or illness of a partner, the founder, or a key employee. Whatever the challenge, a time will come when you, the business owner, leader and guiding spirit, will need to muster the resources to meet what appears to most an insurmountable challenge. These challenges are inevitable, and often there will be more than one in the life of the company. These are the times of grit. They are the events of transformation. Deal with the challenges by confronting the brutal facts. The facts will lead to transformation. Speak directly to the adversity and how, with the commitment, support and the assistance of everyone, the organization will sustain and prevail.

Share in your Mythic Story the process of transformation along with the realization that change is unavoidable, as well as essential for the survival of the company. The Parsifal myth describes how he transforms from the fearless fool to a brave and wise warrior. If you reflect on your history you may find a parallel or similar story in your past. Sharing this part of your story demonstrates your ability to adapt, change, and create continuity. It also sets the expectations for your employees on how to deal with hardship and unexpected loss. And, when we are summoned to reach deep into our being and with full measure, restore the zeal, commitment to excellence, and the right action to sustain ourselves and the business.

Share Your Story

Sharing your story is an act of sacredness. It is an expression of your Spiritual Objective. It provides the basis for your business to operate. A shared Mythical Story sets the parameters and definitions for the behaviors that will empower your business and those who work in it. The Mythical Story is the guiding light by which employees will navigate the daily rituals of doing the business at hand. It gives meaning and purpose to the people who actually do the work. It provides a focal point in the hard times and it is the sustenance of the good times.

As you begin the process of sharing your Mythic Story with employees, suppliers, clients and customers, be forewarned. Along the pathway are unexpected hardships or loss. At these crossroads you will be summoned to reach into yourself and tap your spiritual resources and draw upon the spirit of the business. In these hard times take right actions that will sustain your success and commitment to the process of becoming the entrepreneur. As you share your story and vision of the future, you may find that long time friends and employees protest. Negative response is a potential barrier to the desired outcome and purpose of sharing your Mythic Story. Your story may set new standards and expectations of behavior unacceptable to some in your company. You may find yourself questioning your own wisdom and good judgment. You may discover that those you have depended upon in the past leave you to stand alone because they fear the accountability of the changes you are making. Hold fast. The purpose of sharing your Mythic Story is to make clear the spirit and purpose for doing business. As you move gracefully through the actions of creating your story, we remind you that all things — yes, all things are sacred.

Stories, Legends and Myths

Dan Robertson left his job as an administrator of Municipal Parks and Recreation in Phoenix, Arizona, in 1991 to launch a new business installing rubberized surfacing for municipal playgrounds, churches, and schools. Here is the story Dan wrote about his company. In it you will find all of the elements of a great myth. In this story, Dan defines the spirit of the business, shares how he was called to the adventure, distinguishes the core values of the organization and the ways by which it transforms itself by facing adversity, and addresses the ability of Robertson Industries to renew itself. In between, the lines Dan sets the tone of the business environment and sets the expectation of behavior and commitment. In the final paragraph Dan makes explicit the rewards and outcomes of success. His statement is his formula of success. Finally, Dan keeps the story above the limitations of world-views and focuses attention on the spirit of his company. It is a great myth, a great story. Dan writes:

By 1990 I had been working in the Municipal Parks and Recreation business for twenty years. I had achieved a fair amount of success in my chosen field as well as the respect of my peers. It was my intention to continue in this field and retire when the time was right.

It was during this time that I was offered a job with a Texas company that manufactured and installed resilient rubberized surfacing. This was a huge decision for my wife and me, but after much thought and prayer we decided to begin a new adventure working in private industry.

I opened an office and began selling rubberized surfacing. I hired a Production Manager who had worked for a friend of mine in the construction business. Together we began learning how to install a rubber and urethane system. A friend of mine who had worked with me during my Parks and Recreation days joined us as sales manager. He later brought on board one of his former employees who began working with the Production Manager in the installation side on the business. With this nucleus we sold and installed rubberized surfacing, while all the time wearing a lot of different hats in order to get the job done.

In 1991 the company that we worked for in Texas went out of business. We were all now out of work. It was at this time I decided to start my own company selling and installing resilient rubberized surfacing. I had never intended in my wildest dreams to own a business and was never trained to do so. But I had no choice, I needed a job and so did my employees. On July 1, 1991, Robertson Industries, Inc. was born.

The first six months were a struggle since we had to find new suppliers for the materials we needed as well as finding new customers for our new playground safety surfacing. We had *no references since we were brand new and had only our past reputations and our willingness to work hard. For the first five years we lost money, but in 1996 we made a profit, a small one, but still a profit.*

In 1995 we were joined by an Office Manager who brought much needed organization to the office and a Financial Manager who brought some financial stability and financial awareness to our team.

In 1997 I began a Business Development Process (with Thunderlight Resources) to completely reorganize the company. As a result of the many changes in our business operations, we lost the majority of our employees in the spring of 1999. However, like the mystical Phoenix Bird of mythology, we rose from the ashes and experienced a record year for our company.

Today, Robertson Industries, Inc. installs resilient rubberized surfacing throughout the United States. We also have installed projects in Canada, Mexico, Japan, and Singapore. We are well known by our competitors and respected in the industry. Our customers know us as a company that provides a quality product installed by skilled and dedicated workers and a company that will respond in a positive way to their requests for help.

The Strategic Purpose of Robertson Industries is to create in the hearts and minds of our community and the world at large a vision of a company that cares about the welfare of its employees, the quality of its products and services, and the honesty and integrity of its business relationships.

The following story is from our friend Gary Jackson, President and CEO of Concord Companies, Inc. Notice how Gary embeds into the company story the elements of myth.

*C*oncord Construction Company began in Mesa, Arizona, in 1972. Its roots go back three generations to a small town in Iowa, where the grandfather of Concord's founders built a reputation for fine craftsmanship and honest dealings. It is these standards that live in Concord Companies today.

Concord means "with unity" and was born when its founder, Jim Jackson, perceived a need for capable and efficient construction services. Shortly thereafter, Jim's brother Gary joined the firm. Having acquired construction experience at an early age, the Jackson brothers had their grandfather's excellent example to follow, and quickly developed a long list of satisfied customers. They developed a solid foundation of trust that fostered steady growth for nearly 3 decades.

Concord has evolved from humble beginnings to a statewide enterprise offering wide variety of construction and development services. Concord has built virtually every type of project: office buildings, corporate head-quarters, industrial buildings, schools, churches, retail, medical, and high-density residential projects as well as renovation and rehab jobs. From its offices in Mesa and Tucson, Concord uses its extensive experience, quality craftsmanship, and honest dealings to make each and every project a success. Our clients and vendors continually tell us that we are one *of the finest general contracting firms in Arizona.*

Concord's friendly and enthusiastic employees work "with unity" toward a future of trusting relationships and successful projects. We are not just doing well, we are doing "Great." Just as Becky, our receptionist, who exemplifies the spirit of Concord, come join our family of clients, vendors and employees. See for yourself that Concord is a company of people you can trust.

All things are sacred. And so make every thing you do in your life and business sacred. Be sacred to your Spiritual Objective and Mythic Story.

To close our thoughts about the creation of your story, the Mythic Story of your business, we turn to the insight of George Lucas in his modern epic, *Star Wars*. In the movie *The Empire Strikes Back*, young Luke Skywalker is sent to the Degaba System to be taught the ways of the Jedi Knight. Luke lands his X-wing fighter in a dark, dank, and haunting swamp where it seems to be permanently and inexorably stuck. There, he meets the ancient sage Yoda, who through his teachings, exercises, and encouragement, exposes Luke to his spiritual core, fears, and the power of the "Force."

Yoda teaches the young Jedi how to utilize the Force to move objects, lift crates of supplies, and stack rocks. Luke is distracted by his intuition and fearing for the well being of his friends, Princess Leia and Han Solo, loses his concentration, his pile collapses in a tumble.

Exhausted, Luke looks up only to be discouraged when he sees his transportation, the X-wing fighter, sink into the murky depths of the swamp. Luke complains, "We will never get it out."

Yoda responds, "So certain are you. Always with you it cannot be done. Hear you nothing that I say?"

"Master, " Luke retorts, "moving stones is one thing, this is totally different."

"No. No different. Only different in your mind. You must unlearn what you learned." Yoda advises.

"All right! I will give it a try." Luke despairingly comments.

"No. Try not. Do or do not. There is no try." Yoda admonishes.

After miserably failing to extract the X-wing fighter from the swamp, Luke stomps off in disgust at his inability to utilize the Force fully. Yoda calmly draws upon the Force to raise the fighter from the swamp and place it at Luke's feet. Astonished, Luke exclaims, "I don't believe it."

Yoda responds gently, saying, "That is why you fail."

Chapter Summary
Key Points

• Creating and understanding your myth is a sacred activity

• By choosing to go on an adventure you must explore the duality of the dynamic tension of your inner self and the reality of your outer self

• A shared mythical story sets the parameters and definitions for the behaviors that will empower your business and those who work in it.

• Let your story emerge from your inner self and write with enthusiasm.

Seven Components for creating your Myth:

• Declaration of Spirit
• The Call to Adventure
• Creating the Environment
• Formula for Success
• Slaying the Dragons
• Core Values
• The Experience of Transformation

Questions:

1. What is one thing you need to do to become the hero of your Mythic Story?

2. What right actions did you take today of which you can be proud?

3. What are your core values and beliefs?

4. How does the lesson, All Things are Sacred, apply to your life and business?

Notes for the Spirit of my Adventure:

NOTES - 3. Peter M. Senge, *The Fifth Discipline, The Art and Practice of The Learning Organization*, page 141

    4. Joseph Campbell, *The Power of Myth*, page 5

    5. J. F. Bierlein, *Parallel Myths*, page 5

    6. J. F. Bierlein, *Parallel Myths*, page 5

    7. Kathleen Noble, Ph.D, *The Sound of the Silver Horn*, p. 6

5
Myth and Leadership
Respect and Maintain the Differences

At the moment you made the decision to become a business owner you also made the decision to be the leader of your enterprise. Leaders, like mythological heroes, are courageous, skillful, and committed to excellence. They embrace the challenges in their Mythic Story. The key to effective and potent leadership lies in your willingness to become the entrepreneur, to move between myth and reality, and to allow your Spiritual Objective, Mythic Story, and Strategic Vision to guide and influence the Reality (processes, procedures and practices) of managing the business. To be an effective leader, your primary task is to become the hero of your mythic story. As the business owner, the leadership position is yours. You own it, and you can't escape it. You cannot separate yourself from the responsibility. You are the person to whom everyone will look for guidance, direction, coaching, and approval. The way you assume the crown of leadership will profoundly impact the performance of your business. Leadership is about you.

Leadership is the action of shared being. It is the fine art of sharing your Spiritual Objective and Mythic

Story so that implementation of your Strategic Vision drives the Reality of doing your business. The behavioral components of powerful leadership are influence, emotional intelligence, trust, and competence. These components of leadership are dynamic, requiring continuous refinement, adaptation and maturation. Skill is the magnitude by which we measure performance of the four leadership components. A skillful leader provides graceful influence, inspires unequivocal trust, demonstrates emotional intelligence, and shows a certainty of competence.

Components of Leadership

There is an innate strength in the lesson, Respect and Maintain the Differences, and it brings a sense of balance to leadership. Full realization of this lesson bestows upon us honor, grace, and simplicity to our lives. The lesson instructs us to allow all things to be as they have chosen and respect them. If a person is a woman or a man, then allow them to experience their life to the fullest, without your intervention, bias, or preconception. Only intervene if requested. If a person is black, white, yellow or red, then so be it. Respect the life choices each person makes, observe, learn, and only if you choose, become alike or similar. You are not burdened with the need to make others like yourself. You are only responsible for changing your life. Unburdened by the ways of others, you are freed to live to your fullest measure.

As a leader, this lesson will lead you to occupy a space of wisdom, compassion, and choice. This lesson gives you full freedom to influence, trust, be emotionally intelligent, and competent.

Influence

Influence is your ability to get people enthralled, fascinated, and absorbed by your Strategic Vision. Harry A. Overstreet comments, "The essence of all power to influence lies in getting the other person to participate." To influence presupposes a purpose. To be influential implies that you have a vision that you are committed to accomplish in a measurable way. In the context of your enterprise the "purpose" is your Strategic Vision, which will manifest in the Reality of doing the business. By necessity, your Strategic Vision is conceptually larger than any goal or objective. Your Strategic Vision provides the people doing your business clarity of purpose and the opportunity to participate in bringing it into fruition.

Persuasion and inspiration buttress your ability to influence. Persuasion is your ability to clearly define the features, advantages, and benefits of accomplishing the Strategic Vision. Inspiration is the stimulation that creates excitement and commitment to the spirit and greater purpose of the Strategic Vision.

Discover your Strategic Vision and document it in concise articulate language that is easily understood. Most likely you already know your vision; however, you may be keeping it locked up inside of you. Get it out and share it. Remember you are the leader and the leader is you. For people to follow you they must know what you are thinking and how it affects them. Take action, the right action, and put in motion the activities that define what is really important. Your Strategic Vision is the tool that will propel your enterprise, above all others, now and in the future. Its purpose, once shared, will incorporate into the business environment a common mission with a foundation for decision-making that will benefit both you and all the people in your company. The fundamental concept upon which the Strategic Vision is based is that a company will only be able to flourish if everyone is "on the same page" using the same "best business practices" for managing his or her work. Share your Strategic Vision with high energy, excitement and enthusiasm, and you will be influential in the most positive of ways.

Recognize also that influence is a two-way street. The most powerful way to get people enthralled is to listen to them. The ability to listen actively to a person is a powerful talent that positively influences and inspires a person. Respect the thoughts, inspirations, and inventiveness of those you lead. Let them express themselves. Help them see how their ideas fit into the Strategic Vision of your business. Lead people to do the right things at the right time for the right purpose.

Emotional Intelligence

Adaptation of the lesson *All things are sacred* to the practice of leadership advises that leadership is sacrosanct. Your behavior is revered, honored and appreciated only if you are pure of intention and sacred with your Spiritual Objective. All of your behavior must flow into action and be unwaveringly consistent with your Spiritual Objective. As the leader you will be constantly scrutinized by the people you lead. They are searching for strength and resiliency, which will be reflected in your consistency, honesty, compassion, patience, and willingness to listen. Violate any of these characteristics and you risk the loss of loyalty and erode your capacity to lead. To be a respected leader you must utilize your intuition, control your emotions, and conduct your behavior wisely. To accomplish this, create an environment in which people feel safe with you, so that they can consciously choose to demonstrate behavior that will have the most positive effect on your business.

Daniel Goleman in his book, co-authored with Richard Boyatzis and Annie Mckee, *Primal Leadership: Realizing the Power of Emotional Intelligence*, gives us insight into the behaviors of effective leaders by defining emotional intelligence. Goleman and his colleagues define the four dimensions of emotional intelligence as Self-Awareness, Self-Management, Social-Awareness, and Relationship Management — each with a set of its own competencies. Goleman observes that these competencies "are not innate talents, but learned abilities, each of which has a unique contribution to making leaders more resonant, and therefore more effective." [8]   Working to explore and develop your emotional intelligence will have a profound impact on your leadership skill, and the research demonstrates that there will likely be a positive impact on the financial results of your business.

Self-Awareness, as a domain, is defined as three competencies. Emotional self-awareness is the ability to be responsive to your emotions and to recognize their impact on those around you. It also addresses the ability to maximize your intuition to guide your decision-making. Understanding and knowing your own strengths and limitations is defined as accurate self-assessment. It is about knowing yourself, how you develop, and how you maintain a constant vigil of assessment as you change, mature, and grow. Self-Confidence is your sense of worth and capability.

In the domain of Self-Management, we find the leadership competencies of emotional self-control, transparency, adaptability, achievement initiative, and optimism.

Controlling negative emotions and impulses is essential, as well as being transparent with your honesty, integrity, and trustworthiness. Your flexibility and adaptability to changing environments and business conditions, as well as your skill with overcoming the obstacles and challenges in the path to your goals, comprise the skills of adaptability. Your sense of achievement, the inner desire to improve performance within yourself as well as those you lead, is the road to excellence. Initiative is your ability to capitalize on opportunities, take the right action, and your strategic readiness to positively influence any situation. Optimism is your willingness to see the positive in all circumstances and events.

Empathy, organizational awareness, and service to others are the competencies in the domain of Social-Awareness. The ability to sense the emotions of others, seek understanding of their perspective, and take an active interest in their concerns are the behaviors that characterize being emotionally involved and empathetic. Accurately comprehending the organization, its politics, processes, and decision networks is your organizational awareness. Meeting the needs of your employees, the people you lead, customers, clients, and vendors demonstrates your sense of service.

Relationship Management is the last of the four emotional intelligence domains. Inspirational leadership is your ability to motivate those you lead with a vision of the future that is attractive and compelling. Being persuasive and encouraging people to work with you for the common good of the group are the competencies of influence. Developing others through coaching, feedback, counseling, and mentoring, and finding ways to help them improve are elemental to high quality leadership. Finding new directions, enabling, taking the initiative, and constantly moving towards excellence are the change catalysts. Actively engaging in conflict management to bring resolution to the issues is key to relationship management. Cultivation of relationships and active maintenance of a goal-oriented network of people demonstrate your skill at creating bonds. The skills that promote teamwork and collaboration speak to your ability to build teams between the members of your staff and create cooperation among them.

Trust

Trust emerges from the process of respecting and maintaining the differences. For the dynamic leader the lesson is self-evident. Skilled and sensitive leadership understands the power of diversity and nurtures it. The diverse talents and skills of your employees are the collective mother lode of creativity in your business. The more you can develop the faith and trust in your ability to respect and maintain differences to the greater good of the whole, the more your employees will be inspired and motivated to work towards the ideals of the Strategic Vision. The key behavior is to develop trust.

Trust happens when people have confidence in your leadership. Trust evolves when people can predict with relative accuracy your responses to most or all situations. Trust is the response to your consistency. Trustworthiness is demonstrated by your workers' collective response to your consistency. When people know how you will respond to day-to-day situations in the operation of your business or in crisis, they will trust you. Your task is to develop trust through understanding, not necessarily, through agreement. People may not agree with you, but they will trust you if you are consistent. Uniformity in your process of decision-making, ingenuity, imagination, and the success of your business acumen comprise the fabric of trust. Woven into this fabric is your ability to maintain honest straightforward communications, clarity of direction, and the consequence of action, both positive and negative. Being beyond reproach with your integrity and harmonious with your congruity solidify the intrinsic knowing by the group that you lead by doing the right action in the best interest of the organization. As you maintain your consistency you will nurture the trust of clients, customers, and employees. When the critics come, as they surely will, the group will stand behind you and follow your leadership.

Competence

Individual and organizational competence begins with you, the leader. Your competence is reflected throughout the enterprise as your managers demonstrate their ability to make things happen in a positive proactive way. It is your competence that builds the team, supports the interest of the group and assures the success of your business. High-performance leaders lead high-performance teams. Developing your leadership competencies by actively improving your skills sends a clear message that will result in improved performance of your company. Align yourself with your Spiritual Objective and share the Mythical Story of the company. Lead by creating environments in which people can self-actualize, develop their competencies and maximize their contributions to the business within the boundaries of the Strategic Vision.

Set the stage for success by creating a climate that encourages competence, growth, personal development, creative contribution, and excellence. Climate may not make the business, but it goes a long way toward assuring the health and well being of the business. In an analysis linking a proactive climate to business performance, by David McClelland, the results demonstrated that "in over 75 percent of the cases, climate alone accurately sorted companies into high versus low profits and growth."[9]

Goleman's analysis suggests that "how people feel about their company can account for 20 to 30 percent of the business performance."[10] Competent leadership is the key to creating an environment where working is fun, challenging, and rewarding — it goes straight to the bottom line in higher profit performance. To quote Goleman, in conclusion, "Roughly 50 to 70 percent of how employees perceive their organizations can be traced to the actions of one person: the leader. More than anyone else, the boss creates the conditions that directly determine people's ability to work well."[11]

The Call to Action:
Strategic Vision, Navigation, and Poise

Begin By Documenting Your Strategic Vision

Making your vision of the future explicit is the art of conceptualizing the vision of your company, its purpose and the way it will progress forward. Once documented, the Strategic Vision becomes the benchmark from which all behaviors in the business are guided and directed. It is a statement of purpose, scope, and objective. A well thought-out Strategic Vision is dynamic and always predicts a future. It is the state of being that your company strives to actualize. Always remember that when the future arrives it becomes the present.

What is important is that you document your Strategic Vision and make it known to all of the employees, clients, customers, and vendors in your business. Make clear the goals and objectives, both tangible and intangible, which move the company toward the manifestation of the Strategic Vision. Establish a set of key indicators and the appropriate methods to monitor them to assure success. Empower the team members in your business to get a sense of direction based on the Strategic Vision. Provide them with opportunities to match their thinking to principles of the Strategic Vision. In doing so, they can make appropriate mindful adjustments in their thinking, have a distinct impression of the future, and devote their attention to making it happen.

The Strategic Vision creates a universal source of accountability for all who participate in the Reality (procedures, processes, and practices) of doing the business. Commitment to the essence and spirit of the Strategic Vision promotes the fulfillment of excellence.

There are many ways to access the future. Commonly we typically use words to describe the future that imply sight or vision. Many of us, however, simply are people who do not think visually. If you are one of these people, despair not. Some of us are kinesthetic and feel our way into the future. People who are highly kinesthetic have a sense of how it should be but very little sense of how it should look.

Others of us are highly auditory and talk to ourselves about the future. Regardless of how we access the future, visually, auditorily, or kinesthetically, most of us have the capacity to do so and become dynamic leaders.

Resident between your Strategic Vision and the Reality of doing business are gaps. A gap is an anomalous activity or behavior that does not serve the Strategic Vision. Hold your employees accountable to close and eliminate the gaps. Emphasize accountability to the Strategic Vision. Each employee, as a part of the business team, must be able to rely on others to do what is expected with consistency. Hold people accountable to that end by setting standards for performance. Success in any endeavor is only possible when there is commitment to it. Give your employees the opportunity to be successful by serving the Strategic Vision.

Navigation

In the United States Navy, as well as in all sea navigation, when the captain orders the ship underway, the navigator draws a line on a sea chart from the point of embarkation to the destination. The line from point A to point B is called the track. The captain also orders the acceptable limits of variation from the track. It is the responsibility of the crew to monitor the movement of the ship and keep it on the course determined by the track. Many variables affect the ship's ability to maintain its course and speed. Wind, currents, and wave action all have influence on the ship's movement and speed. Using satellite or sextant, the crew works to maintain heading, speed and course as ordered. Managing the crew's performance is the primary function of the officer of the deck that has, in Navy terms, the "Conn." By constantly monitoring the position of the ship in relationship to the track, the crew makes the necessary adjustments to keep the ship within acceptable limits and on course. The captain is notified if for any reason the ship wanders off course beyond the specified limits of performance.

Like the ship's captain, as the leader of your business team, you have the responsibility to determine the track of the company (Strategic Vision) and set the acceptable limits of deviation from the course. Set these limits in such a way that they can be measured periodically. In the event the business gets off track, or varies significantly from your Strategic Vision, empower your team to take corrective action and notify you of any adjustments to get back on the track, your Strategic Vision.

Leaders set the course for organizations by accessing and giving definition to their concept of the future. In his best selling book, *Good to Great*, Jim Collins says, "Yes, leadership is about vision. But leadership is equally about creating a climate where the truth is heard and the brutal facts confronted. There's a huge difference between the opportunity to have your say and the opportunity to be heard. The good-to-great leaders understood this distinction, creating a culture wherein people had a tremendous opportunity to be heard and, ultimately, for the truth to be heard." [12]

Leadership Composure

Gerber's concepts of leadership are straightforward and succinct. He suggests that leadership consists of three key components: vision, action and spirit. He defines vision as your dream that you will make into reality. It is a dream that you communicate precisely with high energy and a strong sense of commitment. The commitment is reciprocal. All of your employees must understand your vision and align their commitment to making it happen. Gerber warns "Unless you have a clear vision for the future of your business and an equally clear vision for the path you will take to get there, you won't get there except by accident." [13]

Vision, action, and spirit are the essence of leadership, but they must be your vision, your action, and your spirit. In order to construct a strong foundation for success and for the development of your own potential, you must commit yourself to a system of procedures, practices, and processes (that we call Reality), which are proven to be effective in the implementation of your Strategic Vision. These systems are the foundation of the future and will make your enterprise work effectively, efficiently, and consistently. By documenting your Strategic Vision in clear concise unmistakable language, members of your team will be able to focus on giving clients, customers, vendors, and strategic alliances the very best products and services.

Respect and maintain the differences. Do so by organizing your company around your Strategic Vision. Create an environment that encourages each employee to synchronize with the meaning and substance of the vision. Encourage employees to find more effective ways to deliver on the promise of the Strategic Vision and to succeed at their work accountabilities. No one knows how to improve a procedure or process more than the person doing it.

Seek the creative diversity of your people and empower them to make suggestions and innovations that improve the business process, products and services. Inspire them. Energize them to be imaginative and creative, and to become a part of the solution to the challenge of making your business a great place to work. Expect a high level of commitment and participation.

As the leader of your business, create a climate in which the truth can be heard. Always be ready to listen. Help each employee to see how his or her goals fit with the Strategic Vision of the company. Treat your people well. Respect that they too have visions for their lives. They have honored yours, the entrepreneur, by choosing to align their dreams with your vision. Reciprocate by respecting and maintaining the differences. It is your adventure, so be true to it. Be inspirational. Always be moving toward your Strategic Vision. Take the step between. Become the leader. Become the entrepreneur. Thrive between your Spiritual Objective, the Mythic Story, and the Strategic Vision and Reality of the business. When you do, your leadership will be unforgettable.

NOTES   8 Goleman, Boyatizis, Mckee, *Primal Leadership, Realizing the power of Emotional Intelligence*, p. 17

9 David McClelland, *Identifying Competencies with Behavioral-Event Interviews*, Psychological Science, p. 9

10 Goleman, Boyatizis, Mckee, p. 38

11 Goleman, Boyatizis, Mckee, p. 17

12 Jim Collins, *Good to Great*, p. 74

13 Michael Gerber, *E-Myth Mastery Program*, Module 1, p. 1

Chapter Summary
Key Points

- Leadership is about you and your Strategic Vision

- Leadership is the act of shared being

- Document and share your Strategic Vision

- Apply the Four Lessons and the components of leadership:

  Lesson 1: Influence

  Lesson 2: Emotional Intelligence

  Lesson 3: Trust

  Lesson 4: Competence

Questions

1. Are you the leader or merely the most senior employee?

2. What is the current foundation of your leadership system?

3. What characteristics of leadership do you need to develop?

4. What is the current climate of your business?

Notes for the Spirit of my Adventure:

6
Celebrating the Myth
Only the Earth and Sky last forever —
Make every day a good day to die.

Celebrations and rituals have been a part of our human culture that can be traced back to our ancestral beginnings. From the earliest moments of human development, ritual events set the patterns of behavior for the day, week, month, or year. On a larger scale, usually dictated by seasonal changes, spiritual events, a successful hunt, or an important commemorative moment in the history of the tribal community, ceremonies marked transitions. Both ceremony and ritual are important to us because they enrich our lives and mark important passages in the process of living.

It is the process of living that calls us to celebrate. Carl Hammerschlag and Howard Silverman in their book, *Healing Ceremonies*, address the meaning of the words, ritual and ceremony. "Generally, both words refer to processes that separate the ordinary from the extraordinary. Some of the processes are repetitive (we call these rituals) and others may be performed only on special occasions (we call these ceremonies)."[14] Rituals and ceremonies are the events that nourish our potential to live life to its fullest capacity. They are the reminders of our significance in the scheme of a great mystery. They challenge us to do our best. *Only the earth and sky last forever, make every day a good day to die.*

In our fast-paced world, with its expectations for high-speed production and instantaneous gratification, we have little time for reflection and ordained moments to applaud our accomplishments or transitions. Increasingly our culture diminishes the importance of ceremonies and rituals that can make the passages in our lives more meaningful. Ironically the very celebrations and rituals we reject are the ones that sustain our culture. They are the events that authenticate our cultural existence, affirm the cultural myth, and bring to attention an individual's or a group's accomplishments or the completion of a cycle. They are the celebrations and rituals that mark the pathways and passages through growth and maturity, which bring into fruition the fullness of life.

These celebrations and rituals are potent reminders to those of us who have made these passages ourselves, on the same pathway, along with the challenges mastered and the subsequent responsibilities and expectations of wisdom upon their completion.

In our modern social structure the decline of celebrations and rituals that give us meaning is quietly and inexorably eroding the spiritual base of our culture, our communities, our businesses, and our families. The evidence is all around us. Nearly 10% of the new businesses started in the United States fail in their first year and nearly 50% are gone by year five. Just fewer than half the marriages in the United States end by the fifth year as well, and over 70% of second marriages end in only three years. The wedding ceremony has been trimmed from a celebration of spiritual connection and life-long commitment to merely a very expensive party. Bright students are embarrassed to receive the valedictorian award, as it brings attention to their intellect, which in many situations has become a liability among their peers. Attendance at graduation ceremonies for colleges and universities is down. College and universities either require attendance to graduate or beg their students to attend the ceremony.

This cultural movement to forsake ritual and ceremony is also reflected in our businesses. Success in business, with the accomplishment of major company milestones, pass by with barely "a high five" as the next project and the ever-increasing demand for higher profits and performance relentlessly consume our time, attention and lives.

Culturally we are losing our sense of sacredness.

The importance of ceremony in a culture is well documented and etched in our history. Ceremony dates back to the earliest times of indigenous peoples. There are many lessons we can learn from understanding the importance of ceremony and how it relates to myth. Seasonal changes, becoming a man or a woman, and discovering and connecting to a spiritual mate are all events marked by ceremonies woven into the fabric of cultural myths. Fundamental to the structure of ceremony is the notion of how transition relates directly to the cultural myth. Ceremony commemorates the completion of a passage along a specific pathway for the group or individual. On an individual level, ceremony affirms the initiation of a person into the next level of responsibility and accountability in the culture. Completion of the passage moves the initiate from one level of status into higher status, expectation, and esteem. It marks the time when a person can no longer be what he or she has been, and the ritual harkens the change to the new responsibility. A ritual is the enactment of a myth. By participating in a ritual, you are participating in a myth.

Inside the cultural myth of your business is an opportunity to create pathways, passages and ceremonies that will sustain your Mythical Story, celebrate accomplishments of groups and individuals in meaningful ways, and reaffirm the commitment of the people working in your organization. As your business and the individuals inside it go through stages of growth, find ways to ritually celebrate the accomplishments through the passage and along the pathway.

As you become the entrepreneur and occupy the space between your Spiritual Objective, Mythic Story, and the Strategic Vision, carefully construct the pathways, passages, and ceremonies for yourself, your managers, and employees which will mark the deeds of accomplishment in the reality of doing the business.

Pathways, Passages, and Ceremony

Pathways	Passages		Ceremony
Challenge	**Responsibility**	**Expectations**	**Ritual**
Real	Well Defined	Contributing	Social Events
Requiring	Requiring Trust	Sustain	Values
Investment	Requiring	Clear	Honors
Physical	Competence	Mature	Alignment
Emotional	Requiring		Rewards
Outcome Based	Consequence		
Meaningful			
Age/Position			
Appropriate			
Involving Risk			

(Row label on the left: **Elements**)

John McAlister and Elizabeth Potter
October 1999

The Pathway

The process of creating effective developmental pathways, passages, and ceremonies begins with clearly defining your notion of pathway. A pathway is a well established program or curriculum that, when followed, gets a person from a present state to a future state with greater wisdom, skill, and acumen. The pathway is simply point A to point B. Start here, follow this path, and end there.

Imagine for a moment a new employee who enters your organization by first having participated in a recruiting program and successfully satisfying the requirements for employment. Embedded in the recruiting program is the presentation of information the new employee needs to understand about your company: who you are, what you do, why you do it, and what it can mean to them. On the first day of work, the new employee enters a comprehensive training program designed to develop skills and teach systems, standards, and behaviors that will allow the person to be successful within the scope of the position. The pathway is the linear course through the recruiting, hiring and training program. Point A is a non-employee; point B is a trained employee.

The Passage

The passage is the series of tasks and challenges, within the boundaries of the pathway, designed to create and develop skills or new systems. In business we often refer to the passage as a training program. Inside the passage are lessons and tasks carefully designed to be accomplished in sequence. They are calculated to build competence, aptitude, and efficiency with a new skill, expertise, responsibility, or system. The challenges in the pathway are constructed to teach a new under-standing, oriented towards a specific outcome, expressed as a new skill. By accomplishment, the lessons and tasks create competence and proficiency in the newly acquired ability. Essential elements of the challenges are as follows; they are real, they require an intellectual, emotional or physical investment, they have a specified outcome that can be measured; they are meaningful, they are age or position appropriate, and they allow for the possibility of failure.

Making a challenge real means that the initiate

(the learner) sees its relevance, requires a commitment of physical, intellectual and emotional resources. Those who are selected to participate in the journey along the pathway commit to completing all of the tasks, lessons and challenges by expanding their comfort zones, by moving into their learning zones, and by doing so without entering their danger zone. The lessons along the pathway are repeated until the participant demonstrates sustained ability and confirms adeptness. The lessons taught along the pathway should have a specific outcome that is measurable by observation or qualitative analysis.

The skills that the participant learns, and that the systems have created for teaching along the pathway need to be meaningful in the sense that, by learning and doing, they will enhance the participant's value to the organization, community, family, and self. Successfully completing the tasks and challenges along the pathway should raise self-esteem, and refine ability, expertise, proficiency, and talent.

The challenges along the pathway are obligated to be age and position appropriate within the context of the organization. The challenges should be designed to be sufficiently beyond the learner's skills to encourage development by stretching existing boundaries or limitations. However, setting learning and skill-acquisition expectations too far beyond the learner's existing capacities lead to frustration, disappointment, despair and defeat. This is not good for your business or for the employee. A challenge presented with logic, precision, and an understanding of the skill level of the participant initiates growth.

Growth is the theme of the pathway.

Throughout the passage, the participant is at risk.

There is risk of failure and the loss of possible positive outcomes that could result from the successful completion of the pathway. The level of risk should be well defined and shared prior to beginning the pathway. Making the risk clear creates choices for the participant. The participant should know at the outset, the degree of effort and investment required to accomplish the entire task and to complete the passage successfully. The consequences of success should also be made clear at the outset. Be it greater pay, a promotion, development of a valued skill, or increased importance in the company, the positive outcome should be emphasized before taking the first step on the pathway.

Completion of the passage comes with the anticipation that the participant will exercise the newly acquired skills or maturity in a responsible way. As with all responsibility, it needs to be well defined, with clear boundaries and expectations for performance. The responsibilities granted at the end of the pathway and successful completion of the challenges have behavioral expectations that imply trust, and faith. Confidence and reliance are fair expectations as well. The responsibility is not static, rather it is dynamic, and as it is successfully exercised and demonstrated with right action, the range of the responsibility is expanded as the participant's abilities are seasoned. Making choices and taking actions inside the boundaries of the new responsibility also have consequences. Consequences may have both a positive and negative potential for the individual as well as the business. Acceptance of responsibility encompasses acceptance of consequences. In business we call it accountability.

Attached to the new responsibility are expectations

of contribution, continuity, clarity, and maturity. There is an expectation of contribution to the community, family, or business, which supports its core values and Strategic Vision. The individual with the new skill or responsibility is expected to promote the social well being of the organization, to participate actively in sustaining its success and longevity, as well as give back and share the wisdom acquired by means of mentoring. Fixed in the new responsibility is an implied commitment to sustain the meaning and essence of the Mythic Story and the Strategic Vision. Commitment is confirmed by taking right actions to improve the reality of doing the business within the scope of the responsibility. Finally, there is an expectation of maturity. The person with the new responsibility is expected to develop, change, and improve continuously.

The Ceremony

Whether secular or spiritual, ceremony marks the completion of the passage through the pathway. It is a celebration that honors and recognizes the courage, investment, and effort of the person or group. Ceremonies validate our cultural myths and remind us of our history and purpose.

Ceremony is an event created to honor the completion of the challenges of the passage along the pathway. The ceremonial event is planned prior to the participant's taking the first steps along the pathway. All participants are aware where, when, and how it will occur, so that it is anticipated at the outset of the pathway as the point of completion. Meaningful ceremony is shared with the appropriate community or organization. Whatever the size or constitution of the community, the ceremony includes the participant, the ceremonial leaders, and congregation. It makes no distinction of orientation, race, gender, or ethnic background. Rather, it honors the achievement of the individual or group. A meaningful ritual ceremony has significance to the participant, honors accomplishments, aligns with the challenges of the passage, and bestows reward for achievement all under the auspices of a cultural myth. The practice of ceremony reminds us of our traditions, renews the mythic story, and reaffirms the continuity of the culture. It is the ritual of ceremony that links us together and grounds us in our relationships, and reconfirms the shared identity of the mythic story.

At a lecture at the University of Utah, after hearing about the concepts of Pathways, Passages and Ceremony, the audience was asked to share any rituals or ceremonies they have created in their families. One person stood up and said, "In our family we have a car mitzvah ceremony." He went on to explain that every time a child of the family successfully acquired a drivers' license, the entire extended family went out to dinner to celebrate. They went to the same restaurant at every occasion, and the guests included the immediate family, cousins, aunts, uncles, grandparents, and great grandparents. All gathered together in a ritual ceremony to award car keys to the new driver. Each driver in the family would stand and tell mythic stories of their first automobile, including great grandfather who talked of the transition from buggy to the model T. Each would comment on their driving experience, regaling the new driver with admonishments about the responsibility inherent of being a driver. Stories of accidents, parking tickets, and encounters with police for speeding were shared to clearly warn the new driver of the consequences of misdeeds. Expectations were made clear of the trust, confidence, and maturity anticipated of the new driver. In the end, the keys to the car were awarded to the new driver who was expected to stand before the family and promise to exercise his or her new responsibility with care, competence, and wisdom.

This short story of a Utah family demonstrates the power of *Pathways, Passages, and Ceremonies*. The impact of this process can be far reaching for your business by refocusing on your Mythic Story and improving tangible indicators like productivity, sales, revenue, and profits. The process also targets intangible indicators like employee morale, respect, job satisfaction, and creativity. Viewing the application of these concepts in a broader spectrum opens opportunities for you to abstract its application to your Mythic Story. Whole paradigms of operation and doing business can be transformed and new initiatives created. The following story illustrates the potential of expanding the concept of *Pathways, Passages, and Ceremony* in business.

A large non-profit youth foundation with which we have been affiliated included in their programming a variety of outdoor adventuring curriculum. The adventuring program was originally conceived with the objective to provide young people with a significant leadership experience that encouraged them to grow mentally, physically, socially, and spiritually. The platform for the program included biking, hiking, and canoeing, or a combination thereof, on long trips from two to five weeks in duration. Over the many years of implementation the program developed primarily into a physical experience that emphasized tenacity and endurance, but lost the elements of mental, spiritual, and social growth. The primary element of leadership development was all but eliminated from the program. The adventuring program was on a downward slide losing participants at about a 4% annual rate, bringing into question the value of the program to the organization.

John, with his colleague, Elizabeth (Poppy) Potter, accepted the challenge to re-energize the original objectives of the program, recreate it, and implement changes to renew its value to the participants and the organization. The process of re-engineering the program began by dismantling and deconstructing all of the existing presuppositions, systems, processes, and curriculum of the adventuring program. No holds were barred, everything was open to scrutiny. Our promise was to hold dearly to what was valuable, effective, and supportive of the original objectives of personal development in the program. The discovery process (one on one and group interviews) led us to understand the needs of the participants and program leaders. We discovered the program lacked progression and substance. Substandard equipment was the norm, and the *trips were gender and age mixed, which caused social problems that subverted the goals of the trip programs. Trip leader training was abysmal or non-existent, safety was in question, and logistic support was haphazard at best.*

Armed with the research of what was good about the program and what needed to be changed, we set about the task of clearly defining the pathways, passages, and ceremonies that would embrace the program. The program was restructured with an age progression that spanned four years, eliminating as much as possible the social problems that accompanied mixing people of different ages. When appropriate, gender mixing became integral and intentional to the trip programming. Program trip schedules were set with daily goals of distance to travel, curriculum, and activities. Trip leaders were expected to report on a regular basis as to their progress. Events that hindered or advanced the progress of the group were discussed and adjustments made to get the group back to plan. Supporting the adventuring trips required the establishment of a logistics group responsible for vehicles, equipment, and food supplies. Logistics people were charged with the responsibility of complete support for the groups with 24-hour access. To assure the quality of the equipment, they made necessary repairs and if needed, purchased replacements.

Trip leader training emphasized safety, wisdom, and best practices in the adventuring business. Flexibility was allowed inside the curriculum, but not in the trip plan. Trip leaders' responsibilities were clearly defined and expectations set for their performance. Individual and group performances were monitored as the trip progressed.

Ceremonies were created for the beginning and for the end of each trip. The ceremonies were designed to be meaningful and aligned with the maturity of the group, and were performed by trip leaders and supporting staff. A special end of program ceremony was created for the oldest group. The ceremony bestowed honor and recognized the participant's progress through the entirety of the four-year adventure program. A pre-trip ceremony held the night before the adventure was embedded with the message that, upon completion, the participant could no longer be a part of the adventuring program. Rather, participants were expected to become leaders and share their experiences and abilities as such. Upon return, a community ceremony celebrated the transition from participant to leader. In the completion ceremony, the mantel of leadership with all of its expectations of competence and skill was bestowed upon each participant who made passage through the pathway.

By applying the concepts of Pathways, Passages, and Ceremony, not only did the re-engineering of this program become a huge personal and emotional success for the participants, it reestablished the original objectives of the program and created new myths and legends. On the business side, with a 12% increase in price, the participation the following year jumped 17%.

A similar story comes from a Production Manager of a large printing facility in Kansas, who utilized the principles of *Pathways, Passages, and Ceremony* in the manufacturing arena. The presenting challenge for this manager was to find, justify, and implement cost saving ideas to improve the production process and invigorate a competitive edge that had been slipping. The problem was that there had been no effective method to access the ideas of employees and implement them. As he walked around the manufacturing floor seeking ideas, the manager heard clearly and repeatedly that people had submitted ideas for improved productivity, but in the minds of the employees the ideas were rarely considered or implemented. The prevailing attitude of the employee group was that "management" did not care. Knowing that this was a very real but erroneous conclusion he set out to discover why the many great ideas for improvement had been stymied.

Here is his story as he tells it.

What I discovered, by talking with people, was that our process for communicating ideas was seriously flawed at many levels. Like most companies, we had placed suggestion boxes in various parts of the plant. The process required the filling out of a rather complex form with the idea or suggestion. Periodically somebody, no one was ever sure who, would empty the suggestion boxes and give the ideas to the department managers most likely to be interested in the idea. Most of the suggestions were attempts at humorous complaints about managers and suggestions as to how people thought their talents might best be utilized by our competition.

Plain and simply, the suggestion box process did not work. The suggestion form was way too complex, not only asking for a detailed description of the idea but also for financial justification, which the people with the ideas lacked the skills to determine. If a suggestion was submitted in written form or verbally, the implementation of the idea became the responsibility of the front line manager who received it. Front line managers saw their priorities as the day-to-day activities for meeting production goals and schedules while maintaining an exceptionally high quality standard required by the business. Any idea that got to their desk was quickly put into the priority stack, usually at a "B" or "C" level. If it was a really good idea it might be discussed with other front line managers, but rarely justified or implemented. Ultimately, most of the ideas sat at low levels in the priority stack forever. Or worse yet, during a lull in business activity, a manager would implement a good idea and get the credit for it. In addition, the suggestion box was a long-standing icon of the company, a sacred cow; it would not be easy to change.

"Not long after identifying this problem, I was on a business trip to Orlando, Florida. On the return trip, I arrived at the airport unusually early for my flight, and was wondering in and out of the concourse shops, mindlessly burning time until I could board my flight. I saw in one of the shops a curio with two Orca whales on a piece of burl wood. I thought about buying it, all the while arguing with myself to justify the cost. It was an expensive piece, but I got

attached to it and purchased it anyway. It was a long flight back to Kansas, and I kept looking at my new purchase. I wondered how I would explain this spontaneous purchase and the expense to my wife, who I anticipated would not find this curio as interesting or attractive as I did. Then the idea came to me: O-R-C-A could become an acronym for Operational Cost Reduction Assurance and we could make these gifts, like trophies, for anyone who came up with a great idea that we implemented.

So I hid the Orca whales from my wife and took them to work the next day. I showed the burl trophy to my friend Joe and asked him what he thought of my idea. Being a seasoned front line manager Joe was skeptical at first; however, he quickly got excited about the potential of changing the way we processed suggestions and improved our plant productivity.

I asked Joe to take leave of his front line management position, as we had been actively involved in training new managers, and we needed a place to put trainees to give them management experience. I promised Joe he could have his position back in six months, after we implemented our idea. We set Joe up in a quiet office and tasked him with eliciting ideas from our employee group, and if we could cost justify them, get appropriate approval, and then implement them. In this way employees with an idea could talk with Joe. He would complete the suggestion form and document the idea, and test its feasibility. If the idea had the required return on investment, Joe would make it happen.

At the time we made the decision to implement an idea, Joe would go to the weekly department meeting of the employee with the idea and present the Orca whale trophy. We made it a lot of fun and shared our appreciation with the employee's peers. A good friend of mine, Bob, was the Senior Vice President of Manufacturing at the time we implemented the ORCA program. When I shared this idea with him he became very excited. I asked him to sign congratulation and appreciation letters that would be sent to the employee's home. He agreed, so whenever we gave away the Orca whales, Joe and I would compose a letter explaining in detail the idea, how it saved us money, and our appreciation. Joe would mail the appreciation letter to our headquarters and Bob would sign it and send it to the home of the employee. It was very nice, because now the family of the employee would know about the idea we implemented, but also how our company appreciated the contribution. And, of course, whenever the Senior Vice President of Manufacturing came to the plant for a visit, we would make sure Bob made personal contact with our celebrated employees. If a group of employees came up with an idea, we gave them all Orca whales and sent letters to their homes.

For those ideas that could not be afforded or justified, Joe would go to the employee's department manager and arrange a meeting where the three of them would discuss the idea and explain why we would not implement it. There he would present them with a letter explaining our decision in detail. The meeting was documented as a positive effort to improve our process and put into the employee's personnel file. Even ideas that did not work were appreciated, and making the effort to be creative had a positive impact on the employee's performance evaluation.

This program was so successful that we implemented over $1,000,000 of cost saving ideas in the first year. All of these ideas returned their investment within our guidelines of 18 months. Our people really got excited about the process and how we held in high esteem people who came up with workable ideas. Joe found swimming pool toy Orca whales, filled them with helium so that they would float around the department of the employee who came up with the idea. It was a lot of fun and very successful."

This story shows how *Pathways, Passages, and Ceremony* can have a positive impact on your company and raise the esteem of both individuals and the employee group, as well as improve performance. In this example, the pathway is the process of getting ideas from the people who can have the greatest impact. The passage is the process of justifying and implementing the idea. And the ceremony is the feedback loop to acknowledge the implementation of the idea. It is powerful and effective.

Utilizing the process of *Pathways, Passages, and Ceremony* puts into motion a program of continuous improvement focused on the Strategic Vision. Additionally, it hones the reality of getting the business done, so that elegance is matter of fact. As Gerber says "business development is a continuous cycle of innovation, quantification, and orchestration. Innovation is the creation of systems, or the improvement of existing systems. Quantification is putting numbers to the impact made by business systems and tracking their performance over time. Orchestration is the elimination of discretion, or choice in your business systems — doing it the way it's supposed to be done, predictably every time — until innovation improves it." [15]

Pathways, Passages, and Ceremony improves performance and commitment, and values your employees' contributions to the success of the organization. Sincerely honoring accomplishment builds self-esteem, sustains your Mythic Story, and confirms core values, streamlines business processes, and improves the bottom line. It is a process that continuously moves you and your business from myth to reality. It is a principle that can move you toward becoming a successful entrepreneur in the spirit of your adventure.

NOTES   14. Carl Hammerschlag, and Howard. Silverman, *Healing Ceremonies,* page 3.

15. Michael Gerber, *E-Myth Mastery Program,* Module 1, p. 7

Chapter Summary
Key Points

• Only the Earth and Sky Last Forever, Make Every Day a Good Day to Die
• Inside the cultural myth and everyday environment of your business is the opportunity to celebrate.
• Your business and most important asset, people, will go through stages of growth. Celebrate the small and large victories along the path.
• Utilize the concepts of *Pathways, Passages and Ceremony* to improve performance and commitment, and to value your employees, managers, and owners.

Indicators Influenced by Celebrating the Myth:
- Productivity
- Creativity
- Revenue
- Profits
- Morale
- Respect
- Job Satisfaction

Questions:

1. How does your company currently celebrate employee growth and accomplishment?

2. What pathways are well defined in your company?

3. What passages for innovation, quantification, and orchestration already exist in your company?

4. What is one thing you would like to celebrate that could have an amazing impact on your business and your life?

Notes for the Spirit of my Adventure:

7
Myth to Reality
The Thunderlight Experience

E very small business, at some point, will expand beyond its owner's comfort zone. When the business reaches this point the owner is at risk, spiritually, emotionally, and financially. It is incumbent upon the business owner to make a change. This is the time to accept the adventure, get out of the quest, and become, in the very essence of its meaning, an entrepreneur. Few understand the plight of the hard-working business owner more than we do. In fact, we've made it our business to educate business owners about how to get control of the enterprise. We call it the Thunderlight Experience. Our program is the integration of The Four Lessons with the business philosophy found in the best-selling book on small business, *The E-Myth Revisited.* We listen intently to you, the business owner, so that we understand the truth about the current condition of your business. Then we coach you as to how to make the changes that can lead you to true entrepreneurship. We help you understand how your business can be orchestrated, so that it serves your life. We represent strength and hope through our evidenced-based, results-driven program. An association with the Thunderlight

Experience can help you realize a bright and prosperous future for your business and your life. It will lead you, if you choose to participate actively, to the best of times, both personally and professionally.

In response to the question: "How do I learn to understand and absorb all of this wisdom and transform my business?" we offer you the following seven steps that form the foundation for the success of your business and how to make it serve your life.

1. Commit to learn, experience, and implement the changes in your business for it to serve your life. You must go on an adventure and learn what it is you don't know about your entrepreneurial spirit.

2. Learn, understand and embrace The Four Lessons. They give you the right mind set, the right words, the right plan. After you learn those and they become a part of you, the necessary action steps become clear and simple.

3. Develop your Spiritual Objective.

4. Write the Mythic Story about you and your company.

5. Write your Strategic Vision Statement.

6. Develop your Leadership Strategy, and then create an Organizational Strategy.

7. Celebrate your myth to reality adventure with *Pathways, Passages, and Ceremony.*

Remember, the word entrepreneur means "to take between." To transform yourself into an entrepreneurial person means, for you the business owner, to learn how to occupy and connect the space between your Spiritual Objective, your Mythic Story, and your Strategic Vision and the reality of the business.

Let's get started!

Commit to Education

Challenge yourself to be more successful than you are while simultaneously free yourself to get more enjoyment in life. Accept the imperative to grow and advance your education, so that you can achieve what you desire. Commit the time to explore what is possible and do the required study to bring your potential into fruition. More important than "doing it" is seeking an understanding of the philosophies and practices that orchestrate your business, so that it serves your life. There are many people who want to "do," instead of to "be." Take the time to think and reflect upon yourself so that you understand who you want to "be." Imagine, if after years of working in your business, that you discovered you were working on the wrong thing. You could excuse your behavior by saying you didn't have enough time to think! You have time in abundance: use it wisely and think. The typical business owner starts out doing what he or she loves and does it well enough to prosper. Over time, however, this passion becomes just a small part of what must be done. Too often, that person ends up working in the business — not on it. Our experience clearly suggests that a business owner today works far more than necessary for the returns on the investment, effort, and emotion.

Begin your education by being candid with yourself. Do you ever feel like you bought yourself a job? If your answer is yes, you're not alone; most business owners feel that way. Consider embracing a new mindset and look at your business as a vehicle to give you more of what you want from life. When was the last time you saw your business as a source of stability, ease, contentment, and financial freedom? Imagine this as an outcome at the conclusion of every single day! It is possible. We know people who have done it. It can happen for you. We can help you attain this way of life, and commit to doing the strategic work that will position you between your myth and the reality of your business.

The Four Lessons

1. You are the mystery and the mystery is you. Everything in existence is a manifestation of the one living being we call our Mystery. Get to know your Mystery. Your business is always a reflection of you; know who you really are.

2. All things are sacred. This is a realization that will change your life for the better. Just look around, you will see yourself in every tree, in every river, in every cloud, and yes — in every human being. Go between the myth and reality of your business, and thrive.

3. Respect and maintain the differences. Be responsible only to your decisions, your actions, and yourself. Respect your employees, maintain your differences, and offer leadership, not management. Remember that you only control your vision, so stop

trying to manage your people and lead them.

4. Only the earth and sky last forever, make every day a good day to die. Dance in your myth and dare to go between the myth and reality of your adventure. Be the best, all the time. Settle for nothing less.

The magic inside the Four Lessons is that they fit any context. As you continue to understand them we encourage you to think about how they can fit the situations you deal with on a day-in-day-out basis. From the boardroom to the back door, the four lessons have universal relevance. When we think about leadership, we consider the Four Lessons as influencing emotional intelligence, trust and competence and restate them to make them pertinent to the theme of balanced leadership.

"You are the leader and the leader is you" re-frames the lesson "You are the Mystery and the Mystery is you" into the context of leadership. The implications are that leadership is about you, your ability to effectively influence, and your intimate connection to the leadership position. It bonds you to your Spiritual Objective and offers you the opportunity to live in the full realization that your purpose is to serve it with vision and right action which contributes to the improvement of the world around you.

Adaptation of the lesson "All things are sacred" to the practice of leadership advises that leadership is sacrosanct. Your behavior is revered, honored, and appreciated only if you are pure of intention and sacred in your Spiritual Objective. All of your behavior must flow and be consistent with your Spiritual

Objective. As the leader, you will be constantly scrutinized by the people you lead for consistency, coherence, commitment, balance, and emotional stability, as the source of strength and inspiration. Violate any of these conditions and you risk the loss of the leadership mantel and the erosion of your capacity to lead. You must utilize your intuition, direct your emotions, and conduct your behavior wisely.

Respect and Maintain the Differences. For the dynamic leader this lesson is self-evident. Skilled and sensitive leadership understands the power of diversity and nurtures it. The diversity, talents, and skills of your employees are the mother lode of creativity in your business. The more you can develop respect and maintain differences to the greater good of the whole, the more inspired and motivated your employees will work towards the ideals of the Strategic Vision.

The key is to develop trust.

"Every day we will be at our very best to deliver on our promise with competence" restates the last lesson in the domain of leadership. This context-ualizes the lesson, "Only the Earth and Sky Last Forever, Make Every Day a Good Day to Die," to the practice of dynamic leadership. It makes clear the expectations to be the very best, all the time in all we do, and has the anticipation of excellence.

We challenge you to think about how you can change the wording of the lessons to best fit your business without losing the depth of meaning embedded in them. Try it.

Your Spiritual Objective

S tart the adventure at the beginning, and the beginning is you. If you want a better life, then make a serious commitment to get it. Creating a better life for yourself has nothing to do with your business, until you complete an exploration of your essential character. What are your core beliefs? What kind of life do you want? What do you value? What is your essence? These are the questions you must answer.

Your Spiritual Objective is a statement that expresses your answers to all these questions. It is a declaration about the creator of the business: you. Your Spiritual Objective is about the essential elements, which you know in your heart, define your nature, guide your behavior, animate your daily life, and points you in the direction you are headed. It is not about being a good husband or wife, father, mother, businessperson, or leader. If you are on that path while thinking about your Spiritual Objective, expand the search; go deeper. You'll know when you have it. Your Spiritual Objective is about who you want to "be," not what you want to "do."

Once your Spiritual Objective is written, live with it on your desk at work and in a prominent place at home. Refer to it often throughout your day. See if it defines your leadership, drives your ethics, commitment, and conduct personally and professionally. If it does, it will become the statement of personal objective and the means to measure the success of your adventure.

Your Mythic Story

The next step in the entrepreneurial adventure is creating, writing and documenting your myth, your company story. It is a story that remains a constant beacon throughout your business. It is a story that captures the essence of what you want your business to become. It's a description of what makes your business special. Think about it as a "welcome" statement to your company.

Imagine a client, customer, vendor, or employee just entering the world of your exceptional company. What would your adventure offer them? What do you do that no other company does? What are you passionate about offering? How do you celebrate? What is your philosophy?

It becomes the story you share with employees, vendors, clients, customers, family and friends. Most likely your mythic story already exists; you just haven't written it and shared it yet. Creating your Mythic Story is a straightforward and deliberate process. Most importantly, reveal your Mythic Story with deliberation and intention, then frame it, hang it on the wall for all to see, and share it at every opportunity.

Your Strategic Vision

Writing your Strategic Vision statement will propel your business, above all others, present and in the future. Why? Because most small business owners never make the transition to becoming an entrepreneur. Most owners never define who they want to "be," write their Mythic Story, or document their vision. They keep it neatly wrapped and packed away in their head, thinking its the Holy Grail of control and only for personal knowledge.

Start by detailing a picture of the future — your vision of what the business will look like, act like, and feel like. How will it perform when it is mature? Once you have a sense of the future, then detail it. Describe to yourself the size of the business. Make clear in your vision how the business will operate. Illustrate in your mind how the business will influence the employees' well being and how it will enrich your life. Determine as many details as you can imagine. Write them down and work on it until it is a perfect future. Be mindful, this is not a one-line mission statement but rather a clear written statement of what your business will be when it is mature and complete. Making your vision of the future explicit is the art to creating a mindset of where your company will go and how it will progress.

Keep your vision, heart, and mind centered. Make sure the Strategic Vision serves your Spiritual Objective and aligns with your Mythic Story. Leaders set the course by accessing the future. Document, frame, and hang your Strategic Vision statement where you and others can readily see it. Your Strategic Vision is the foundation of leadership in your company for people to connect to, align with, join and help you achieve.

Leadership Strategy

John Maxwell in his book on leadership states, "Leadership is influence — nothing more, nothing less."[16] We want to take that a little farther. Your Spiritual Objective, Mythic Story, and Strategic Vision combined with influence, trust, emotional intelligence and competence, combine to make the winning formula for leadership in the reality of success.

Your Spiritual Objective, Mythic Story, and Strategic Vision are the first three essential processes of creating a leadership system for your life and business. The next four processes are the characteristics of leadership. Developing your capacity to be influential, to generate trust, to be competent, and to be emotionally intelligent will strengthen the foundation of your company's business and empower your employees to deliver high performance. Together, balanced, and operating in concert, these processes and elements of leadership form the catalyst for accomplishment.

- Influence is your ability to get people involved.

- Trust happens when people place confidence in the leader.

- Dimensions of emotional intelligence exist in the four domains of Self-Awareness, Self-Management, Social Awareness, and Relationship Management and eighteen competencies.

- Competence is the leadership ability to make things happen in a positive, proactive way that builds the team, supports the interest of the group, and assures the success of your business vision.

High performance leaders lead high performance teams in the context of a culture that embraces change. Find the strength and confidence to lead by pursuing ways to improve your leadership skills and competencies. The result will be improved performance throughout your company. Align yourself with your Spiritual Objective, share the Mythical Story of your company, and lead by creating an environment in which people can self-actualize and maximize their contributions to the business within the framework of the processes streamlined to accomplish the Strategic Vision. Make your vision a reality.

Organizational Strategy

An organizational strategy is a key system for you to use to structure the reality of making your business work. The organizational strategy will only work, however, if you remember that the present must be made to serve the future. Create your organizational strategy, as it will appear when you have achieved your Strategic Vision, and begin operating from the basics of that strategy today. The organizational chart represents the structure and responsibilities that will support your Strategic Vision. The chart represents, organizationally, what your business will look like when it is done, how the positions and accountabilities will be organized in order to achieve your vision.

This style of organizational chart is not intended to "box people in" or to create a "power structure." Rather, it is a description of reporting relationships that encourage accountability, while providing everyone with a "personal leader"who can set priorities, resolve conflict as it arises, and who can recognize when to celebrate employee successes.

The purpose of the strategic organizational chart is to demonstrate clearly how each team member fits into the whole of the business structure. The chart exhibits the area for which each team member is accountable, i.e. Marketing, Client Fulfillment, Finance, Manufacturing, and Operations. It is incumbent on all team members to work together in the reality of doing the business and to accomplish the goals established by the company to achieve its Strategic Vision. This system sets the stage for all other management systems that define accountability, and is therefore worthy of spending the time to get it right.

Celebrate

Remember to celebrate your accomplishments large and small. Sustain your company's viability by setting the pathways consciously, clearly defining the task in the passages, and celebrating the accomplishments of individuals and groups. There are many places to look in your company and your life to construct and implement the concept of *Pathways, Passages, and Ceremony.* Consider your business as if it were going through a cycle of infancy, through adolescence, and on to maturity. It is a business ever growing, every expanding. See it as a process of Pathways, Passages, and Ceremony. Look at your business development as a continuous process or opening the hoop of innovation, orchestrating it, quantifying it, and then closing the hoop. Move the operating condition of your business from chaos to order, to a well designed and managed enterprise. Each step of the way, plan the Pathway, Passage, and Ceremony. This is a process long recognized to be an important tool for your journey.

Now the Entrepreneur

N ow you know what you must be prepared to learn. Understanding the wisdom of the Four Lessons will have a commulative effect on growth and success as they fold into the practice of your business. Your well being and the fulfillment of your life depend on your ability to go between your Spiritual Objective, Mythic Story, and the Strategic Vision that guides the Reality of doing your company's business. It depends upon your willingness to forgive the ways of the past, become an entrepreneur, and adopt a new leadership strategy that escorts the way into the future. As a transformed business owner, the entrepreneur of your business, choose to limit your responsibility to just two domains: Vision and Capital. Becoming an "entrepreneur," in its true sense and meaning, will provide you the freedom you have diligently sought and allow your business to serve you.

We return to the Raven's Story, closing the hoop and beginning again. Plant the seeds of good in your life. Like the Raven, have the courage to create personal transformation. Take the steps to move from business owner to entrepreneur. Go into the long house of knowledge, meet the fire of life, and live the lessons to the full measure of your capacity.

This is the Thunderlight way.

NOTE—16. John Maxwell, *The 21 Irrefutable Laws of Leadership*, p. 17

Take Action!
The Business Development Analysis

Now that you've learned the Four Lessons about becoming an entrepreneur, we would like to offer you thoughts and insights into those lessons that are specific to you and your business. All you have to do is complete the business development analysis form located on our website at www.thunderlightresources.com.

Or call us at 800-908-9189.

Complete the business analysis for a FREE coaching session and call us so you can understand what we can do for you and your business. We promise you an inspiring and enlightening session with insights on how to free yourself from the chaos of your business.

By completing this in-depth analysis, you are agreeing to a FREE telephone engagement call with one of our coaches to determine if our services can be of benefit to your business and your personal life. During the call, we'll be happy to answer all your specific questions.

No one understands the plight of the busy entrepreneur better than we do. In fact, we've made it our business to educate other business owners how to get control of their business and their lives through a proven evidence-based development process. We listen intently to understand the truth about the current condition of your business.

What we have found to be true is that most small businesses simply don't work. The people who own them do, and are working far more than they should for the return they are getting.

Results

Once you have read the book and completed the form, your coach will help you analyze the results. First, by identifying specific areas of opportunity to create order in your business, and, second, by helping you discover system solutions as you discuss personal frustrations. Getting free from your business begins with the right mind set, the right words, and the right plan. After you learn those, the necessary action steps become perfectly clear and simple.

The Thunderlight spirit of coaching has produced measurable tangible results for our business owner clients. The program can do the same for you and your business. The Four Lessons are a discipline for personal growth and learning, while the program is a demonstrated business development system. The Thunderlight Experience integrates them into your life and business moving you from Myth to Reality.

Thunderlight Resources, LLC

We offer the business owner, entrepreneur, manager and employee educational products and coaching on the strategy, the art, and the science necessary to achieve one's vision in business and life — a pathway for making sense of transformation and providing programs for the successful implementation of change. At its essence: "Tools for the journey — because it's your life"

Our coaches are passionately committed to producing measurable results, as clients advance and accelerate growth in their lives and their business. Our promise is to engage and educate people with sound principles of how to design a business that serves the owner's life and the well-being of the people who join the enterprise.

Thunderlight Resources presents strategic coaching through a unique business development system. This proven process is largely carried out through bi-weekly telephone coaching calls utilizing over 100 processes centered around leadership, marketing, management, finance, lead generation, lead conversion, and client fulfillment. In addition, the company provides on-site development programs as clients advance through their stages of growth.

The key to becoming an entrepreneur is to go on an adventure and learn what you don't know about the ways your business can serve your life. This is the education our teachers spent a lot of time teaching us: Arising out of our life experiences.

Please visit our website:

www.thunderlightresources.com

to review:

- Our Free Business Development Analysis
- Client Success Stories
- Frequently Asked Questions about our programs
- Sponsoring the Thunderlight Experience; a personal interactive workshop for business owners to advance and accelerate growth in their lives and their business.

For information about Speaking Engagements, Teaching Intensives, and Retreats given by the authors contact:

Thunderlight Resources
P O Box 2854, Carefree, AZ
800-908-9189
www.thunderlightresources.com

Notes:

Recommended Reading
For Your Entrepreneurial Adventure

Leadership

Harai, Oren, *The Leadership Secrets of Colin Powell.* New York, NY: McGraw Hill, 2002.

Maxwell, John C. *The 21 Irrefutable Laws of Leadership.* Nashville, TN: Thomas Nelson, 1998.

Murphy, Emmett C. & Michael Snell, *The Genius of Sitting Bull, 13 Heroic Strategies for Today's Business Leaders.* Englewood Cliff, NJ: Prentice Hall, 1993.

Inspirational

Chopra, Deepak, M.D. *Creating Affluence.* San Rafael, CA: New World Library, 1993.

Covey, Stephen R., *The Seven Habits of Highly Effective People.* New York, NY: Simon and Shuster Publishing, 1989.

Ferrini, Paul, *Love Without Conditions.* Greenfield, MA: Heartways Press, 1994.

Hammerschlag, Carl A. and Howard D. Silverman, *Healing Ceremonies, Creating Personal Rituals for Spiritual, Emotional, Physical and Mental Health.* New York, NY: Berkley Publishing Group, 1997.

Noble, Kathleen, Ph.D., *The Sound of the Silver Horn: Reclaiming the Heroism in Contemporary Women's Lives.* New York, NY: Ballantine Books, 1994.

Ruiz, Don Miguel with Janet Mills, *The Four Agreements Companion Book*. San Rafael, Ca: Allen Publishing Company, 2000.

Quinn, Daniel, Ishmael, *An Adventure of the Mind and Spirit*. New York, NY: Bantam/Turner Book, 1992.

Walsch, Neal Donald, *Friendship with God*. New York, NY G.P. Putnam's Sons, 1999.

Business

Collins, Jim, *Good to Great*. New York, NY: Harper Business, 2001.

Eckes, George, *Making Six Sigma Last*. New York, NY John Wiley & Sons, 2001.

Gerber, Michael E., *The E-Myth Revisited*. New York, NY: Harper Collins Publisher, 1995 (First Addition).

Senge, Peter M. *The Fifth Discipline, The Art and Practice of The Learning Organization*. New York, NY: Doubleday, 1990.

Whyte, David, *Crossing the Unknown Sea*. New York, NY: Riverhead Books, 2001.

Success Strategies

Robbins, Anthony, *Unlimited Power*. New York, NY: Simon & Schuster, 1984.

Kiyosaki, Robert T. with Sharon L Lecter, C.P.A.,*Rich Dad, Poor Dad, What the Rich Teach Their Kids About Money that the Poor and Middle Class Do Not*. New York, NY: Warner Books, 2000.

Bibliography

Bierlein, J. F., *Parallel Myth*. New York, NY: Ballantine Publishing Group, 1994.

Campbell, Joseph, with Bill Moyers, *The Power of Myth*. New York, NY. Broadway Books, 1998.

Gerber, Michael E., *The E-Myth Revisited*. New York, NY: Harper Collins Publisher, Inc. 1995 (First Addition).

Gerber, Michael E., *E-Myth Mastery Program, Module 1: Business Development Process, LD 001*. Santa Rosa, California, Gerber Business Development Corp., 1997.

Collins, Jim, *Good to Great*. New York, NY, Harper Business, 2001.

Goleman, Daniel with Richard Boyatzis, Annie McKee, *Primal Leadership: Realizing the Power of Emotional Intelligence*. Boston, MA, 2002.

Hammerschlag, Carl A. and Silverman, Howard D., *Healing Ceremonies, Creating Personal Rituals for Spiritual, Emotional, Physical and Mental Health*. New York, NY, The Berkley Publishing Group, 1997.

Maxwell, John C., *The 21 Irrefutable Laws of Leadership*. Nashville, Tennessee, Thomas Nelson, Inc., 1998.

McClelland, David, *Identifying Competencies with Behavioral-Event Interviews*. Psychological Science 9, pp 331-339, 1998.

Noble, Kathleen, Ph.D., *The Sound of the Silver Horn: Reclaiming the Heroism in Contemporary Women's Lives*. New York, NY: Ballantine Books, 1994.

Senge, Peter M. *The Fifth Discipline, The Art and Practice of The Learning Organization*. New York, NY, Doubleday, 1990.

Index of Names

Notes

Notes

Notes

Notes

Notes

Notes

Thunderlight Resources
P.O.Box 2854, Carefree, Arizona
Tel (800) 908-9189 • Fax (480) 488-2783
www.thunderlightresources.com

Order Form

Title	Price	x	Qty		Total

Myth to Reality $19.95 _____ = $_____

Shipping & Handling (determined by number of products):
    1=$4.95 • 2 to 5=$8.95 • 6 to 9=$13.95 • 10-15=$17.95
    Continental USA only   = $_____

                              Taxable total   = $_____

                              AZ residents 8.1% = $_____

                              ORDER TOTAL $_____

Date: _____

Payment method: ❑ Check (to Thunderlight Resources)
    ❑ Mastercard   ❑ Visa   ❑ American Express
    Acct number_____
    Expiration date _____
    Exact name on card_____
    Authorization code_____ Date of charge_____
    Signature:

Ship to:

Name/Company _____

Address _____

_____

City/State/Zip _____

Tel/Fax _____

E-mail _____